THE COMBINATION
MICROWAVE COOK

D0539509

THE
COMBINATION
MICROWAVE
COOK

Annette Yates & Caroline Young

A HOW TO BOOK

ROBINSON

ROBINSON

First published in Great Britain in 1997

This edition published in 2015 by Robinson

Copyright © Constable & Robinson 2010

5 7 9 10 8 6

The moral right of the author has been asserted.

A CIP catalogue record for this book
is available from the British Library.

ISBN 978-0-7160-2080-6

Printed and bound in Great Britain by Clays Ltd, St Ives plc

Papers used by Robinson are from well-managed forests
and other responsible sources

MIX
Paper from
responsible sources
FSC
www.fsc.org   FSC® C104740

Robinson
An imprint of
Little, Brown Book Group
Carmelite House
50 Victoria Embankment
London EC4Y 0DZ

An Hachette UK Company
www.hachette.co.uk

www.littlebrown.co.uk

NOTE: The material contained in this book is set out in good faith for general guidance and no
liability can be accepted for loss or expense incurred as a result of relying in particular circumstances
on statements made in the book. Laws and regulations are complex and liable to change, and readers
should check the current position with relevant authorities before making personal arrangements.

How To Books are published by Robinson, an imprint of Little, Brown Book Group.
We welcome proposals from authors who have first-hand experience of their subjects. Please
set out the aims of your book, its target market and its suggested contents in an email
to Nikki.Read@howtobooks.co.uk

CONTENTS

Illustrations *by Lindsay Thomas*

INTRODUCTION

The arrival of the combination cooker in our kitchens means that all those irritating limitations of microwave cooking, like the lack of crisp golden-brown crusts on cakes, pies, roasts and many more dishes, are a thing of the past. Now we have the perfect answer – the appliance which combines all the advantages of microwave cooking (speed, ease of use and compactness) with hot air and/or a grill to produce the crisp and browned appearance that we expect. In addition, the ability to switch from one method – defrosting, microwaving, roasting, baking or grilling – to another, sometimes without even having to remove the food from the oven, makes the combination cooker the most useful appliance in your kitchen.

The combination cooker will give you the result every cook aims for – perfectly cooked, appetising food with the minimum of fuss and time. For today's cooks, with so many demands on their time, this must surely be the one appliance they can't afford to be without.

We are both working wives and mothers, juggling the myriad activities that we and our families are involved in, yet with a keen interest in food and in eating healthily and well. By using all the capabilities of our combination cookers, we are able to produce attractive and delicious meals in a fraction of the conventional cooking time – whether we are just cooking for two or for the whole family. An added bonus is the ease with which combination cookers can be kept clean – no bending or kneeling down to reach inside them!

This book explores combination cooking to the full – for those of you with a combination cooker that has a fan-assisted hot air system and for those of you who use a microwave with built-in grill. For cooking with microwaves only, the companion books to this publication – *Microwave Cooking Properly Explained*, and *Microwave Cooking Times at a Glance!* – contain cooking techniques, recipes and time charts.

Like us, you will, in time, wonder how you ever managed without a combination cooker. First though, we do suggest that you spend a little time reading our notes on what cookware we use and how we have developed the recipes. We want you to have successful results from the very first recipe you try. Lastly, since we hate cleaning cookers as much as anyone, we also recommend that you read our suggestions on taking care of your combination cooker, with the aim of it never getting very dirty to start with!

We hope you enjoy both cooking and eating these recipes!

Annette Yates and Caroline Young

1

THE COMBINATION COOKER

WHAT IS A COMBINATION COOKER?

Knowing just what a combination cooker is, and how it works, makes it easier to use. Incidentally, we choose to use the word 'cooker' and not 'oven' because we feel its capabilities are far greater than those of an 'oven'.

A combination cooker combines microwave energy with hot air, or with radiant heat from a grill, to cook and brown food simultaneously. It can, of course, be used to cook food with microwaves only. Most models can also be used to cook with hot air only (as in conventional ovens) or with grill only. Let's look at each cooking method individually.

MICROWAVE

Microwaves actually penetrate the food, attracted by its moisture, fat and sugar content. The molecules in the food agitate rapidly, causing friction, and it is the heat from this friction that cooks the food. As it is a very quick and moist form of cooking, the outer layers of the food are not browned or crisped.

Cooking by microwave only is ideal for fish, sauces, fruit and vegetables (both fresh and frozen), pasta, rice, grains and pulses, sauces, soups, steamed puddings and preserves. It is also very useful for all those fiddly jobs you would otherwise do on the hob – melting chocolate or butter, blanching vegetables or liquefying ingredients like honey or jam.

Microwave energy alone is also used on the defrost program on your model.

CONVECTION

This is the traditional method of cooking food by hot air which may or may not (depending on your model) be circulated by a fan. Other models use the radiant heat from the grill element to heat the oven cavity. The compact size makes it very cost-efficient for cooking small amounts by convection only.

Small and individual food items such as biscuits, scones, rolls and small cakes should be cooked on convection only. They are so small that, if they were cooked on combination, the microwaves would overcook them before they had a chance to brown. Very rich fruit cakes are also best cooked on convection only.

GRILLING

Grills operate with the door closed and the turntable (if fitted) rotating to give even browning. They can be preheated before use.

We recommend grilling thin chops, hamburgers, bacon and gammon rashers, thin fish portions, sandwiches and 'things on toast' such as Welsh Rarebit.

COMBINATION – MICROWAVES WITH HOT AIR

This cooking method combines the use of microwaves (reducing the cooking time by around 50 per cent) with hot air (browning and crisping the surface of the food) to give dishes the traditional appearance, texture and taste that we expect. Some combination cookers use an element behind the back wall of the oven cavity to heat the air. A fan may also be fitted to circulate the air evenly. Other models use the radiant element of the built-in grill to heat the air. With some foods, the end result can be even better than with conventional cooking. Cakes will rise beautifully, with an excellent texture. Roast meats and poultry are crisp and golden brown, yet remain moist and succulent as a result of the reduced cooking time. For the same reason, meat shrinkage is also reduced.

Combination cooking is very successful for cakes and sponges, casseroles and 'au gratin' dishes, pies and flans, desserts such as crumbles, roast vegetables, scone rounds, breads, roast meats and poultry.

MICROWAVE + GRILL

This cooking mode combines the radiant heat from the grill with microwave energy. The heat from the grill heats the air in the oven cavity as well as giving concentrated radiant heat to the top of the food. The grill operates with the door closed and the turntable (if fitted) rotates to give even browning. The grill can be preheated before use.

This method is excellent for cooking dishes which need gentle heating throughout and a golden brown top (such as potato-topped dishes and baked pasta like lasagne). It's also good for thick portions of fish, meat or poultry, possibly coated with breadcrumbs, which grill to a crisp finish while a low microwave power level shortens the cooking time to keep the meat or fish moist and tender.

PRE-SET PROGRAMS

Models vary in their number and type of pre-set programs. Most will include special programs for jacket potatoes, roast meats and poultry, re-heating convenience foods and for defrosting. The manufacturers' handbooks give specific instructions for each individual model so you will not find them in this book.

COOKWARE

Like most cooks, the amount of storage space we have in our kitchens is at a premium, so we have slimmed down the amount and type of cookware we use to the minimum. Each cooking mode on the combination cooker has different requirements from the cookware used. Here is a brief run-down.

MICROWAVE cookware must allow the microwave energy to pass easily through it and into the food. This obviously rules out anything metal (which reflects microwaves) and any dish decorated with gold, silver or any other metallic paint. The microwaves will cause the metal in the decoration to spark and blacken (called arcing), certainly spoiling the dish and possibly damaging the cooker too. Thick pottery often absorbs some of the microwave energy, becoming very hot and slowing down the cooking. Unglazed pottery absorbs water during washing which, in the microwave, may expand into steam and crack the dish. Do not use fine glass, polystyrene, plastic dairy containers (they will melt), recycled paper products (they may contain minute metal particles) or dishes repaired with glue (it will also melt).

CONVECTION cookware can be any conventional oven-proof items including metal cake tins and baking sheets (but remember, if your cooker has a turntable, it has to be able to turn).

GRILL cookware should be flameproof and may include metal (again, if your cooker has a turntable, make sure it can rotate easily).

COMBINATION cookware has to allow microwave energy to pass through it for maximum efficiency yet be able to withstand high temperatures. We like the versatility of ovenproof glass which enables you to switch from one cooking method to another using the same dish.

We have a very basic collection of various sizes of oven-proof glass and ceramic glass casseroles (with lids), soufflé dishes, bowls, jugs and deep, straight-sided flan dishes. The soufflé dishes are 18 cm/7 inches and 23 cm/9 inches in diameter and the flan dishes are 20 cm/8 inches and 23 cm/9 inches in diameter and 5 cm/2 inches deep. Casseroles with lids are particularly useful – if the lid needs to be vented (to allow the steam to escape and prevent boiling over) we just slip a wooden cocktail stick between the lid and the rim of the dish. Wide rims or handles make for easy lifting. We also use several shallow ceramic gratin dishes, both individual and family-sizes. These usually have no lids so, when a cover is needed, we slip them inside a microwave bag or (for combination cooking) a roasting bag.

In addition to microwave and roasting bags (available in various sizes), other disposables we find useful are heavy-duty food (freezer) bags for microwave use only (not the thin polythene variety), microwave paper wrap and non-stick baking paper (the last two are very useful for lining the bases of cake dishes).

For the best results, we recommend you use the standard set of measuring spoons (¼ tsp, ½ tsp, 1 tsp and 1 tbsp). They are inexpensive and available from cookware shops or supermarkets. We also find a wire balloon whisk very useful for making super-smooth sauces.

When a dish size isn't specified, always choose a container slightly larger than you would use for conventional cooking, to prevent the food boiling over. This is especially important when cooking rice or pasta and foods with a high liquid content, such as soups, and fruit cooked in syrup.

Some manufacturers suggest in their cookbooks that you can use metal baking dishes when cooking on combination. If you have such a model and wish to use a metal dish please remember that all our cooking times are developed using ovenproof glass dishes which allow the microwaves to enter the food from all angles to shorten the cooking time. With metal dishes you will need to increase the cooking time and the final texture and appearance of the dish may be affected.

Remember, all cookware used for combination, convection and grilling will get very hot – always have some oven gloves handy.

TAKING CARE OF A
COMBINATION COOKER

Keeping a combination cooker clean does take a little more effort than a microwave. The oven lining gets very hot so food can burn on, but it is still a lot easier than cleaning a conventional cooker – if only because it is at counter top height!

The most useful tip we can give you is not to let the oven cavity get a build-up of grease and food spills. When possible, we cover the food, at least for the first part of the cooking time. This generally gives better results and also minimises splattering on the oven lining (which usually occurs during the first part of the cooking, before moisture has evaporated and before the food has begun to form an outer cooked crust). Use a vented lid (an easy way is to tuck a wooden cocktail stick between the lid and the rim of the dish) or make a couple of small cuts in a microwave or roasting bag – this will allow the steam to escape and prevent any boiling over. We use roasting bags for cooking joints of meat or whole poultry, using a size which is large enough to enclose a roasting rack too.

However, some spills or splattering are inevitable and the answer is always to wipe them up immediately – certainly before using the cooker again. This avoids any build-up of food which, when the cooker is next used, would harden and make it more difficult to remove. Wipe the oven lining with hot soapy water, then rinse and dry it thoroughly. To loosen any stubborn food, bring a bowl of water to the boil on microwave mode. Adding some lemon slices to the water, before heating it, will help to dispel any lingering stale smells. The resulting steam and condensation will soften the food and make it easier to remove. If that fails, use a little smooth cream cleaner on a soft cloth (it is important to avoid scratching the oven lining.) Then dry the inside of the cooker well (dry it too after cooking foods such as pasta or rice which make a lot of condensation).

Turntables and accessories should be washed frequently with hot soapy water and dried well before putting back into the cooker.

It is important to keep the door seals and locks clean and to avoid damaging them in any way. Doors are fitted with safety locks and, if damaged, they will prevent the cooker from operating.

Position the cooker so that the vents in the outer casing are not obstructed. Always plug it directly into a wall socket – do not use an adapter. Some models can be built into a wall unit but do check with the manufacturer first. Clean the outer casing with a soft cloth and warm soapy water – do not allow any water to seep into the vents.

Avoid using a kettle in such a position that, when it is boiling, the steam is directed into the vents.

Remember, the interiors of these cookers get hot and the outer casings get warm. Always use oven gloves.

Following these simple tips will keep your combination cooker looking fresh and clean for years.

GETTING PERFECT RESULTS

As well as being great fans of combination cookers, when it comes to the end result we have very high standards. Any recipe we test that isn't at least as good as, preferably even better than, the conventionally-cooked version is discarded. Good results also rely on good ingredients, no matter what cooking method is used.

Why not buy fresh food in season? It will most certainly have travelled less, will have far more flavour and be less expensive. Shop little and often, especially for fruit and vegetables, and use them quickly. When shopping for small quantities, consider buying packs of ready-to-use items such as vegetables and salad. With absolutely no waste, they can work out less expensive than buying, for example, a whole cabbage – the remains of which are discovered days later lurking in the bottom of the fridge!

With **fresh fruits and vegetables,** we have assumed that you will prepare them ready for cooking – new potatoes can be scraped or scrubbed, baking potatoes are left with the skins on, unless otherwise stated, onions and garlic are peeled. Choose small to medium-size items such as leeks, parsnips and carrots – they will have more flavour.

Most **herbs** are available fresh all the year round, those sold in pots being the best value. Well watered, they will last for a couple of weeks on the window-sill and are handy for snipping off a leaf or two as required. Vacuum-packed herbs need to be kept refrigerated and, once opened, used very quickly. Chop or scissor-snip leafy herbs such as parsley and chives. Basil is tender and should be torn with the fingers (it will blacken if chopped). Woody herbs like thyme and rosemary should be stripped from the stems. Alternatively, use a whole sprig during cooking and remove it from the dish before serving. Tubs of frozen chopped herbs can be used straight from the freezer – just shake out the amount required and quickly return the remainder to the freezer. Jars of freeze-dried herbs have a good colour and flavour and should be kept in a cool, dry cupboard. **Whole dried spices** keep their flavour, whereas ground spices lose their flavour rapidly so buy in very small amounts, keep them in tightly closed jars and in a cool, dry cupboard.

We are continually aware of the need to keep the fat content of our diets to a low level and, indeed, this is made easy with a microwave or combination cooker. You will find that, in our recipes, we use the minimum amount of oil and fats. At the same time, we make no excuses for using good quality **olive oil, butter** and the occasional dollop of **cream**. As we use so little, the cost is low but the difference it makes to the final flavour of the dish is worth every penny and every calorie! If you are a vegetarian or simply prefer to use other fats and oils, the recipes will of course work with one exception. When a recipe specifies butter or block margarine or soft tub margarine, it is important to the final result to use exactly the type listed. When using oil in a cake recipe, choose one with little or no flavour such as grapeseed or sunflower oil. Don't waste extra virgin oil in cooking – it should be used in dressings or just sprinkled over food.

Full-fat, semi-skimmed and skimmed milks are interchangeable, unless the recipe states otherwise. We use semi-skimmed for good flavour and its lower fat content. Low-fat hard cheeses are fine in place of the full-fat versions when melted in a sauce. However, their lack of fat means that, when used on top of a dish, they do not give a rich brown finish. We prefer to choose a well-flavoured mature cheese and use less of it. Parmesan cheese or Pecorino cheese is best bought in a piece and either grated or finely chopped in a food processor. Store it in a tightly-closed jar in the refrigerator. Those bags of ready-grated Cheddar, Mozzarella and other varieties of cheese you see in the stores are useful – you can use some of the cheese, reseal it and store it in the fridge or freezer. Frozen cheese can be shaken from the bag directly into hot dishes, without thawing it first. Do use only **double cream or crème fraîche** for cooking, unless otherwise specified. Creams with a lower fat content become very thin when heated and yoghurt usually separates. When using a reduced-fat crème fraîche, check that it doesn't contain gelatine as a thickener, or it will become very thin during heating.

Our recipes use dried **pasta** and white **rice** (unless otherwise stated). If you prefer to use fresh pasta, remember it needs a very short cooking time – check the packet instructions and adjust cooking times to suit. Unless the recipe specifies otherwise, cook pasta and rice uncovered. Use a large bowl or casserole and hot liquid (use boiling water from the kettle). Pasta should be covered with boiling water by at least 5 cm/2 inches. Stirring occasionally prevents the pasta sticking together in clumps. Add a pinch of salt and a dash of oil if you wish, though we find it unnecessary. A standing time is important after cooking for the pasta to absorb water and soften. You can cover the bowl with a thick tea-towel to trap in the steam. Cooking rice is foolproof if you use the method where the rice grains absorb all the liquid to become plump and tender. Don't be surprised if you find that, at the end of the cooking time, not all the cooking liquid has been absorbed – just cover the bowl and leave the rice to stand for 5 minutes when it will finish cooking and absorb the liquid. Brown rice can be used in place of white in most of the recipes but you will need to increase both the amount of liquid used and the cooking time. Most brown rice needs about 750 ml/1¼ pints liquid to 115 g/4 oz rice and a cooking time of about 25 minutes.

Some excellent ready-to-use **chilled** or **frozen pastries** are available. Some so good that no-one would know you hadn't made them yourself. Shortcrust pastry, both plain and sweet, puff pastry and filo pastry are all useful to have to hand. We have included (on page 137) our favourite press-in pastry – definitely no rolling out is required and it can be made by hand or in the food processor. When time allows we like to make up a dry pastry mix in the food processor, tip it into a freezer bag and store it in the refrigerator or the freezer. We use 450 g/ 1 lb plain flour, a pinch of salt, 55 g/4 oz chilled butter or margarine and 55 g/4 oz chilled white fat. Cut the fats into cubes, put all the ingredients into the processor and buzz until the mixture resembles fine breadcrumbs. To use it, mix in, with a fork, just sufficient cold water to make a soft dough (3–4 tbsp to a half-quantity of the above dry mix). To line a 20 cm/8 inch flan dish use approximately one-third of the dry mix; for a 23 cm/9 inch dish, use about half of the mix.

There are several other items we find very useful. Small jars of **ginger purée, red or green pesto, garlic and tapenade** are very useful, just a teaspoonful can instantly add lots of flavour to a casserole, rice and pasta dish. Once opened, keep it in the refrigerator. **Spray cans of vegetable** and **olive oil** are excellent for giving dishes a very light coating of oil – much easier than using a pastry brush. We prefer **curry paste** to curry powder because it gives a smoother and richer taste to a dish. Choose a mild or hotter variety, depending on your taste. **Sachets or cans of partly cooked rice** can fill an empty space in a menu in minutes – we add extra flavour with chopped herbs, melted garlic butter, a teaspoonful of curry paste or a good squeeze of lemon juice.

Other good seasonings are the fiery **hot pepper sauce,** called Tabasco, and the sweet, yet hot, **chilli sauce.** Use both with caution to begin with – you can always add more! The addition of even a dash of wine to a dish adds a subtle and delicious flavour but, once opened, wine should be used up very quickly. We solve this problem by keeping a bottle of **dry white vermouth** in the fridge – it has a longer life and makes an excellent alternative. When red wine is needed, look for the 25 cl cans which are readily available.

Three things we are really fanatical about – **freshly milled sea salt**, **freshly milled peppercorns** and **real vanilla extract**. Admittedly, real vanilla is more expensive than vanilla flavouring but you need to use very little to enjoy that wonderful flavour and aroma. We also tuck one or two **vanilla pods** into a jar of caster or granulated sugar to perfume and flavour the sugar, ready for sprinkling over fresh fruit, natural yogurt or for using in recipes. We also like to have a selection of canned tomatoes, beans and vegetables such as artichoke hearts available, as well as frozen fish, shellfish and vegetables.

Don't Forget
All cookers, including conventional gas and electric models, vary in their performance. Do read the manufacturer's instruction booklet which accompanies your cooker. After you have used your own combination cobker for a short while, you will become very familiar with the way it behaves. Use the times we give in the recipes, check the result in the conventional way and cook for a little longer if necessary. Individual tastes vary and only you know how well-cooked you like your vegetables or how brown the top of a pasta dish should be. When testing a dish, if it is cooked but not as brown as you would like it, simply continue cooking with temperature or grill only. If the food starts to bubble over during cooking, leave the temperature as it is and reduce the microwave power level slightly for the remaining time. At the end of the given time, check the result – you may need to add a few minutes more. Note down any changes you make or, next time you prepare that recipe, use a slightly larger dish.

Some recipes, such as cakes and pastries, cook best if they are put into a hot (preheated) oven. You will notice that, in the recipe methods, we sometimes give an instruction to 'preheat the oven to . . .'. In other words, the oven *must* be hot before you start cooking, so don't forget to preheat it. In other recipes, such as casseroles, the dish can go into the cold oven and then start to cook in a rising temperature + microwave power. Similarly with the grill – sometimes we suggest preheating before putting the food under it. Where no preheating instruction is given, simply pop the food in the oven and switch on MICROWAVE + GRILL.

When cooking a two-serving dish on MICROWAVE + GRILL stand the dish on a high rack and cook as the recipe directs. When cooking the same recipe for four servings it is preferable to stand the dish on a low rack and cook for the given time – this allows the dish to heat up properly without getting too brown on top. The power and efficiency of grills vary considerably from model to model so, to avoid burning food, keep an eye on dishes under the grill.

A final word on ingredients! For best results, please use metric or imperial measurements – do not mix the two.

ABOUT THE RECIPES

The recipes in this book have been developed in 800–900W microwave + grill and combination cookers with the following power levels.

HIGH	800–900W	100%
MED-HIGH	550–675W	Approx. 70–75%
MEDIUM	400–450W	50%
MED-LOW	250–325W	Approx. 30–35%
LOW	125–225W	Approx. 15–25%

If your combination cooker has a wattage higher than 800–900, you may need to reduce the power level to one which is equivalent to that used in the recipes; then cook for the time given. If the wattage is lower, simply cook for a little longer than stated in the recipes.

Make full use of the power levels and temperatures on your model. If you find that a dish is cooked but not brown enough, cook for a little longer on convection only. If a dish is brown enough but is not cooked through, turn the temperature down and continue cooking with the same microwave power. If a dish starts to bubble over, continue cooking with the same temperature, but lower the microwave power and cook for a little longer. With cookers becoming more powerful always cook for the minimum time given and then check and cook a little longer if necessary.

SYMBOLS

All the recipes in this book can be cooked in a combination cooker. The majority of them can also be cooked in a MICROWAVE + GRILL model. These symbols are sure to prove useful as a quick reference.

m+g means the recipe is suitable for MICROWAVE + GRILL

c means the recipe is suitable for COMBINATION

SERVING QUANTITIES

As you will see, we have given alternative serving quantities in many of the recipes. In these, the quantities which serve 4, and the cooking times for these larger quantities, appear in *italics*.

INGREDIENTS

Please use metric or imperial measurements – for best results, do not be tempted to mix the two.

All spoon measures are level, unless otherwise stated (do use a standard set of measuring spoons – see page 13).

2

SNACKS AND STARTERS

Many snacks and starters are quick to make in the microwave-only. With the addition of a grill or with combination cooking, the range can be extended to include crisp-baked dishes such as samosas, pizzas, spiced potato wedges with crunchy skins, and 'things on toast'.

Keep useful items such as flour tortillas, pizza bases and canned vegetables such as beans and tomatoes on hand and you will be able to rustle up tasty snacks and starters in minutes.

VEGETABLE SAMOSAS

Serve hot or cold, as a main dish or a snack. Good for a packed lunch.

Serves 4

1 small onion, finely chopped
1 garlic clove, crushed
1 small carrot, finely chopped
1 small potato, finely chopped
1 tsp oil, plus extra for brushing
1 tbsp medium or hot curry paste
1 tbsp lemon juice
1 tbsp tomato purée
40 g/1½ oz frozen sweetcorn
Freshly milled salt and pepper
4 large filo pastry sheets

1. Put the onion, garlic, carrot, potato and oil into a casserole. Cover and cook on HIGH for 5 minutes, stirring once. Stir in the curry paste, lemon juice, tomato purée and sweetcorn. Season to taste and leave to cool completely.

2. Lightly brush one pastry sheet with oil and fold it in half lengthways. Spoon one quarter of the vegetable mixture onto one end of the pastry. Fold the pastry diagonally over the filling, using up the strip to make a triangular parcel. Repeat with the remaining pastry and filling.

3. Preheat the oven to 250°C.

4. Brush the parcels with oil and arrange on an ovenproof plate.

5. Put into the hot oven and cook on 250°C + MED-LOW for about 8–10 minutes or until crisp and golden brown.

EGGS FLORENTINE

To serve 2		To serve 4
225 g/8 oz	**cook-in-the-bag spinach**	*450 g/1 lb*
150 ml/¼ pint	**milk**	*300 ml/½ pint*
1 tbsp	**plain flour**	*2 tbsp*
1 tbsp	**butter**	*2 tbsp*
55 g/2 oz	**grated cheese**	*115 g/4 oz*
	freshly milled salt and pepper	
2	**medium eggs**	*4*

1. Cook the spinach following packet instructions. Drain well, then roughly chop. Divide between individual flameproof dishes, making a hollow in the centre of each. Keep warm.

2. Put the milk into a bowl. Whisk in the flour, then add the butter. Cook on MED-HIGH for about 3 minutes *(4 minutes)*, stirring frequently, or until the sauce just comes to the boil and is thickened and smooth. Stir in three-quarters of the cheese and season to taste.

3. Break an egg into the hollow in each dish. Prick the yolks with a skewer or cocktail stick and sprinkle with salt and pepper. Carefully spoon the sauce over the top of each egg, making sure they are completely covered. Sprinkle the remaining cheese on top.

MICROWAVE + GRILL:
4. Preheat the grill.

5. Stand the dishes on a high *(low)* rack. Put under the hot grill and cook on MEDIUM GRILL for about 5 minutes *(8 minutes)* or until the eggs are just set and the top is golden brown.

COMBINATION:
4. Preheat the oven to 200°C.

5. Put into the hot oven and cook on 200°C + MEDIUM for about 7 minutes *(11 minutes)* or until the eggs are just set and the top is golden brown.

SPICED POTATO WEDGES WITH AVOCADO AND SOUR CREAM DIP

These are ideal for serving as a snack or a starter. Serve piping hot to dunk into the Avocado and Soured Cream Dip.

To serve 2		To serve 4
2	**baking potatoes, scrubbed**	*4*
1 tbsp	**oil**	*2 tbsp*
½ tsp	**ground coriander**	*1 tsp*
½ tsp	**ground cumin**	*1 tsp*
	freshly milled salt and pepper	

1. Cut each potato lengthways into 8 even-sized wedges. Put the potatoes and oil into a food (freezer) bag and seal the opening. Shake until the potatoes are evenly coated with the oil. Add the spices and shake well again.

2. Arrange the potatoes in a single layer on a flameproof plate. Sprinkle with salt and pepper.

MICROWAVE + GRILL:

3. Stand on a high rack. Cook on MEDIUM + GRILL for 8–10 minutes *(10–15 minutes)* until soft and golden brown. Serve piping hot.

COMBINATION:

3. Preheat the oven to 200°C.

4. Cook on 200°C + MEDIUM for *15–20* minutes *(18–25 minutes)* until soft and golden brown. Serve piping hot.

AVOCADO AND SOURED CREAM DIP

To serve 2		*To serve 4*
150 ml/¼ pint	**soured cream**	*300 ml/½ pint*
	freshly milled salt and pepper	
3 tbsp	**finely chopped chives**	6 tbsp
1 small	**avocado, peeled, stoned and**	1 large
	finely diced	
1 tsp	**lemon juice**	2 tsp

Put the soured cream and seasoning into a serving bowl and stir until combined. Stir in the chives, then stir in the avocado and lemon juice.

CHILLI EGGS

Add some crusty bread to mop up the sauce.

Serves 2

390 g can ratatouille
2 tsp sweet chilli sauce or to taste
2 medium eggs
Freshly milled salt and pepper
4 tbsp grated cheese

1. Preheat the grill.

2. Combine the ratatouille and chilli sauce. Spoon into two individual shallow flameproof dishes, making a hollow in the centre of each. Break an egg into each hollow and prick the yolk with a skewer or cocktail stick. Season to taste and top with the grated cheese.

3. Stand the dishes on a high rack. Put under the hot grill and cook on MEDIUM + GRILL for about 3–4 minutes or until bubbling hot, the top is golden brown and the eggs just set.

BEEF AND BEAN POTS

A quick meal – just add some hot garlic bread.

Serves 2

**1 tbsp butter
1 small onion, thinly sliced
2 tsp Worcestershire sauce
2 tsp sweet chilli sauce
447 g can baked beans
115 g/4 oz corned beef, diced
27 g packet crisps
55 g/2 oz grated Cheddar cheese**

1. Put the butter and onion into a casserole, cover and cook on HIGH for about 2–3 minutes or until very soft. Stir in the Worcestershire sauce, chilli sauce, beans and corned beef.

2. Cover and cook on MED-HIGH for about 3 minutes until piping hot.

3. Spoon into two individual dishes and top with the crisps. Sprinkle the cheese on top.

4. Preheat the grill. Stand the dishes on a high rack. Put under the hot grill and cook on MED-LOW + GRILL for 2–2½ minutes or until golden brown.

HOT STUFFED ROLLS

These rolls may be prepared in advance, wrapped and refrigerated. If they are very cold, allow 1–2 minutes' extra cooking time.

Serves 1

1 small sourdough baguette or large roll

BACON FILLING:

25 g/1 oz soft butter
1 tbsp wholegrain mustard
1 tsp finely chopped fresh parsley
100 g/3½ oz finely chopped, lean cooked bacon or gammon
Freshly milled pepper

1. Preheat the oven to 200°C.

2. Cut a shallow lid from the top of the baguette and scoop out the crumbs leaving a 1 cm/½ inch shell. (Use the crumbs in a stuffing or on top of another dish.)

3. Beat the butter with the mustard and parsley, then stir in the bacon or gammon. Season with pepper. Spoon into the roll and replace the lid, gently pushing it on firmly. Wrap in non-stick baking paper.

4. Put into the hot oven and cook on 200°C+ LOW for about 8–10 minutes or until piping hot. Serve hot.

CHARGRILLED CHICKEN AND MAYONNAISE FILLING:

2 slices cooked, chargrilled chicken, flaked
2 spring onions, finely chopped
55 g/2 oz Gouda cheese, diced
3 tsp mayonnaise
1 tsp barbecue relish
Freshly milled salt and pepper

Follow the method above, combining all the ingredients to fill the roll.

RATATOUILLE TORTILLAS

Serves 2

390 g can ratatouille
2 tsp chilli sauce
175 g/6 oz cooked beef or lamb, shredded
Freshly milled salt and pepper
4 Mexican-style flour tortillas
25 g/1 oz garlic butter
55 g/2 oz grated Cheddar cheese

1. Combine the ratatouille, chilli sauce and shredded beef or lamb. Season to taste. Divide the mixture between the tortillas and roll up Swiss-roll fashion. Place in a flameproof dish.

MICROWAVE + GRILL:

2. Put the butter into a bowl and cook on HIGH for about 20 seconds or until melted. Brush over the tortillas. Sprinkle the cheese over the top.

3. Stand on a high rack. Cook on MEDIUM + GRILL for about 5–6 minutes or until bubbling hot and golden brown.

COMBINATION:

2. Preheat the oven to 200°C. Put the butter into the warm oven to melt. Brush over the tortillas. Sprinkle the cheese over the top.

3. Cook on 200°C + MEDIUM for about 8–10 minutes or until bubbling hot and golden brown.

BAKED EGGS WITH HAM AND CHEESE

Serve with hot toast or warm rolls.

Serves 2

1 small onion, finely chopped
1 tbsp butter
85 g/3 oz smoked ham, chopped
1 tsp wholegrain mustard
2 medium eggs
Freshly milled salt and pepper
55 g/2 oz grated Gruyère cheese

1. Put the onion and butter into a casserole. Cover and cook on HIGH for about 1½–2 minutes or until very soft. Add the ham and mustard and stir until combined.

2. Preheat the grill.

3. Spoon the ham mixture into two individual shallow flameproof dishes, making a hollow in the centre of each. Break an egg into each hollow, prick the yolk with a skewer or cocktail stick and season to taste. Top with the cheese.

4. Stand the dishes on a high rack. Put under the hot grill and cook on MEDIUM + GRILL for about 3–4 minutes or until the eggs are just set and the top is golden brown.

BAKED EGGS AND POTATOES   m+g

Serves 2

1 small onion, finely chopped
15 g/½ oz butter
1–2 tsp curry paste
225 g/8 oz cooked new potatoes, diced
2 medium eggs
Freshly milled salt and pepper
55 g/2 oz grated cheese

1. Put the onion and butter into a casserole. Cover and cook on HIGH
   for about 2 minutes or until very soft. Stir in the curry paste and
   then the potatoes.

2. Preheat the grill.

3. Spoon the potato mixture into two shallow individual flameproof
   dishes, making a hollow in the centre of each. Break an egg into
   each hollow and prick the yolk with a skewer or cocktail stick.
   Season to taste and top with the grated cheese.

4. Stand the dishes on a high rack. Put under the hot grill and cook
   on MEDIUM + GRILL for about 3–4 minutes or until the eggs are
   just set and the top is golden brown.

PIZZAS
PIZZA TOPPINGS

The toppings on pages 33–39 will cover three to four 20–23 cm/8–9 inch part-baked pizza bases. Instructions are for assembling and cooking one pizza.

Serve as whole pizzas, cut into wedges or cut into thin strips.

ONION AND ANCHOVY PIZZA

Anchovy lovers may like to replace the olive oil with oil from the drained anchovies.

2 tbsp olive oil, plus extra
450 g/1 lb onions, thinly sliced
3 garlic cloves, crushed
1 tbsp fresh thyme leaves
Freshly milled salt and pepper
Slices of jalapeno pepper, optional
50 g can anchovy fillets, drained and halved lengthways
16 black olives

1. Put 2 tbsp of the oil, onions, garlic and thyme into a casserole. Cover and cook on HIGH for about 7–9 minutes, stirring once or twice, until very soft. Season.

2. Preheat the oven to 200°C.

3. Put one of the pizza bases on a low rack. Spoon some of the onion mixture over the top, spreading it almost to the edges. Arrange a few jalapeno slices (if using), anchovies and olives on top, pushing the olives gently into the onion. Drizzle over a little extra oil.

4. Put into the hot oven and cook on 200°C + MED-LOW for 7–9½ minutes or until golden brown.

ONION, TOMATO AND MOZZARELLA PIZZA

1 tbsp olive oil, plus extra
450 g/1 lb red onions, thinly sliced
1 tbsp finely chopped fresh marjoram
Freshly milled salt and pepper
227 g can chopped tomatoes, drained
225 g/8 oz Mozzarella cheese, thinly sliced
25 g/1 oz black olives

1. Put 1 tbsp of the oil, onions and marjoram into a casserole. Cover and cook on HIGH for about 8 minutes, stirring once or twice, until very soft. Season. Stir in the tomatoes.

2. Preheat the oven to 200°C.

3. Put one of the pizza bases on a low rack. Spoon some of the onion mixture over the top, spreading it almost to the edges. Arrange slices of the cheese and olives on top. Drizzle over a little extra oil.

4. Put into the hot oven and cook on 200°C + MED-LOW for 7–9½ minutes or until golden brown.

TUNA AND ROCKET PIZZA

1 tbsp olive oil, plus extra
1 large onion, thinly sliced
1 garlic clove, crushed
150 ml/¼ pint passata
1 tsp sugar
Freshly milled salt and pepper
Two 200 g cans tuna chunks, drained
140 g/5 oz grated Cheddar cheese
3–4 small handfuls of rocket leaves

1. Put 1 tbsp of the oil, onion and garlic into a casserole. Cover and cook on HIGH for about 5 minutes, stirring once, until very soft. Stir in the passata, sugar and seasoning. Gently stir in the tuna.

2. Preheat the oven to 200°C.

3. Put one of the pizza bases on a low rack. Spoon some of the tuna mixture over the top, spreading it almost to the edges. Sprinkle a little cheese on top. Drizzle over a little extra oil.

4. Put into the hot oven and cook on 200°C + MED-LOW for 7–9½ minutes or until golden brown. As soon as a pizza comes out of the oven, piping hot, scatter some of the rocket leaves on top – they wilt in the heat.

HAM, PEPPER AND PINEAPPLE PIZZA

1 tbsp olive oil, plus extra
1 large onion, thinly sliced
1 medium green pepper, stalk and seeds removed and thinly sliced
4 tbsp tomato purée
1 tsp sugar
Freshly milled salt and pepper
175 g/6 oz ham, shredded
4 canned pineapple slices, drained and chopped

1. Put 1 tbsp of the oil, onion and pepper into a casserole. Cover and cook on HIGH for about 5 minutes, stirring once, until very soft. Stir in the tomato purée, sugar and seasoning.

2. Preheat the oven to 200°C.

3. Put one of the pizza bases on a low rack. Spoon some of the onion mixture over the top, spreading it almost to the edges. Top with some of the ham and pineapple pieces. Drizzle over a little extra oil.

4. Put into the hot oven and cook on 200°C + MED-LOW for 7–9½ minutes or until crisp and golden brown.

PEPPERONI AND RED PEPPER PIZZA

1 tbsp olive oil, plus extra
1 small onion, thinly sliced
2 medium red peppers, stalk and seeds removed and thinly sliced
2 garlic cloves, crushed
2 tbsp tomato purée
Freshly milled salt and pepper
115 g/4 oz pepperoni sausage, thinly sliced
12 black olives
3 tbsp grated Parmesan cheese

1. Put 1 tbsp of the oil, onion, peppers and garlic into a casserole. Cover and cook on HIGH for about 7–8 minutes, stirring once or twice, until soft. Stir in the tomato purée and seasoning.

2. Preheat the oven to 200°C.

3. Put one of the pizza bases on a low rack. Spoon some of the pepper mixture on the top, spreading it almost to the edges. Arrange a few of the pepperoni slices and olives on top, gently pushing the olives into the peppers. Sprinkle with a little Parmesan cheese. Drizzle over a little extra oil.

4. Put into the hot oven and cook on 200°C + MED-LOW for 7–9½ minutes or until crisp and golden brown.

PRAWN AND ITALIAN CHEESE PIZZA

2 tbsp olive oil, plus extra
1 medium onion, thinly sliced
1 tbsp finely chopped fresh oregano
227 g can chopped tomatoes, drained
175 g/6 oz button mushrooms, sliced
225 g/8 oz cooked prawns, thawed if frozen
Freshly milled salt and pepper
175 g/6 oz Bel Paese cheese, thinly sliced
12 pimento-stuffed green olives, halved

1. Put 2 tbsp of the oil, onion and oregano into a casserole. Cover and cook on HIGH for about 4–5 minutes, stirring once, until soft. Stir in the tomatoes, mushrooms, prawns and seasoning.

2. Preheat the oven to 200°C.

3. Put one of the pizza bases on a low rack. Spoon some of the prawn mixture over the top, spreading it almost to the edges. Arrange a few cheese slices and olives on top. Drizzle over a little extra oil.

4. Put into the hot oven and cook on 200°C + MED-LOW for 7–9½ minutes or until crisp and golden brown.

FRESH TOMATO AND HERBS PIZZA

Olive oil
350 g/12 oz ripe tomatoes, thinly sliced
3 tbsp finely chopped fresh herbs – oregano, thyme, marjoram, etc
Freshly milled salt and pepper
175 g/6 oz Mozzarella cheese, thinly sliced
3 tsp grated Parmesan cheese

1. Preheat the oven to 200°C.

2. Put one of the pizza bases on a low rack. Lightly brush with oil. Arrange the tomato slices over the top and brush with oil. Sprinkle with the herbs and add seasoning. Top with the Mozzarella cheese and sprinkle with the Parmesan. Drizzle over a little extra oil.

3. Put into the hot oven and cook on 200°C + MED-LOW for 7–9½ minutes or until crisp and golden brown.

CHEESE RAREBIT AND VARIATIONS

This versatile cheese mixture can be kept tightly covered in the refrigerator for up to one week. Use as suggested below and also see Smoked Haddock au Gratin (page 85) and Cod with Bacon and Cheese (page 87).

Makes 4 servings

4 tbsp plain flour
½ tsp dry mustard powder
4 tbsp milk or beer
225 g/8 oz grated Cheddar cheese
Dash of Worcestershire sauce

1. Put the flour and mustard into a bowl and add the milk or beer. Beat until smooth. Beat in the cheese.

2. Cook on MED-HIGH for 2–3 minutes, beating frequently, or until the cheese has melted and the mixture is smooth and leaves the side of the bowl when stirred. Stir in the Worcestershire sauce.

3. Use as below or cool, cover and refrigerate.

CHEESE RAREBIT ON TOAST

Serves 1

1 thick slice of hot toast
1 portion of Cheese Rarebit

1. Preheat the grill.

2. Put the toast onto a flameproof plate and spread the Cheese Rarebit over the top.

3. Stand on a high rack, put under the hot grill and cook on GRILL until golden brown. Serve immediately.

BACON RAREBIT

Cook the Cheese Rarebit on the toast as on page 40. Serve topped with grilled or fried bacon rashers.

CHEESE RAREBIT WITH POACHED EGG

Serves 1

1 medium egg
1 thick slice of hot toast
1 portion of Cheese Rarebit (page 40)

1. Break the egg into a small dish and prick the yolk with a skewer or cocktail stick. Cook on HIGH for 25–30 seconds or until just firm.

2. Preheat the grill.

3. Put the toast onto a flameproof plate and spread the Cheese Rarebit over the top.

4. Stand on a high rack, put under the hot grill and cook on GRILL until golden brown.

5. Loosen the egg and slide it on top of the Cheese Rarebit. Serve immediately.

CHEESE RAREBIT WITH ONION

Spoon onto hot toast and grill until golden brown. Alternatively, use in recipes as suggested for Cheese Rarebit.

Makes 4 servings

1 tsp butter
1 medium onion, thinly sliced
4 tbsp plain flour
½ tsp dry mustard powder
4 tbsp milk
25 g/1 oz grated Cheddar cheese
Dash of Worcestershire sauce

1. Put the butter and onion into a casserole. Cover and cook on HIGH for about 2 minutes until very soft.

2. Stir in the flour and mustard, then the milk. Beat until smooth, then beat in the cheese.

3. Cook on MED-HIGH for about 1½–2 minutes, beating frequently, until the cheese has melted and the mixture is smooth and leaves the side of the casserole when stirred. Stir in the Worcestershire sauce.

4. Use immediately or cool, cover and refrigerate.

3

VEGETABLES AND VEGETARIAN DISHES

Vegetables are the basic ingredients of the recipes in this chapter and most of them are suitable for vegetarians, or can easily be adapted with simple changes. Where butter is used, replace it with vegetarian spread or oil; choose vegetarian cheeses and vegetable stock. Meat is replaced with vegetarian versions, beans, diced tofu or minced Quorn.

Bags of fresh breadcrumbs, bread cubes and crumble mix are always useful for topping dishes – store them in the freezer and just tip out the amount you need for a recipe (they will thaw very quickly). Bags of grated cheese are another useful stand-by and they can also be frozen. Pumpkin seeds, sesame seeds and crushed nuts also make good toppings.

You will notice that, in some recipes which use microwave + grill, we place the dish on a high rack for two servings and on a low rack for four. You may find that you want to vary this, depending on how quickly food browns in your appliance – keep an eye on it the first time you make a dish.

TOMATO TART

Excellent with a well-flavoured rice or pasta salad.

Serves 4

225 g/8 oz puff pastry
150 g soft cheese with garlic and herbs
375 g/13 oz cherry tomatoes
2 tsp olive oil
Freshly milled salt and pepper
1 tbsp thyme leaves
2 tbsp freshly grated Parmesan cheese

1. Roll out the pastry and cut into a 23 cm/9 inch round. Lift onto a flat ovenproof plate. Lightly dampen the edge. From the pastry trimmings, cut a 1 cm/½ inch strip and place around the edge of the circle to form a rim. Refrigerate the pastry for 30 minutes.

2. Tip the soft cheese into a bowl and warm on MEDIUM for 45–55 seconds or until softened. Stir well.

3. Preheat the oven to 200°C.

4. Place the soft cheese in small spoonfuls over the pastry. Put the tomatoes in a bowl, drizzle over the oil, add salt, pepper and the thyme. Gently stir together to coat the tomatoes then scatter them over the cheese. Sprinkle the Parmesan cheese on top.

5. Put into the hot oven and cook on 200°C + LOW for about 20 minutes or until the pastry is crisp and golden brown.

GARDENER'S PIE

To serve 2		To serve 4
375 g/13 oz	**potatoes, peeled and diced**	*675 g/1¹/₂ lb*
1 small	**onion, thinly sliced**	*1 medium*
2 small	**leeks, thinly sliced**	*4 small*
2	**celery sticks, sliced**	*4*
2 medium	**carrots, sliced**	*4 medium*
25 g/1 oz	**butter**	*55 g/2 oz*
3 tbsp	**plain flour**	*40 g/1¹/₂ oz*
1 tsp	**wholegrain mustard**	*1 tbsp*
300 ml/½ pint	**milk**	*600 ml/1 pint*
55 g/2 oz	**fresh or frozen peas or broad beans**	*115 g/4 oz*
85 g/3 oz	**grated Cheddar cheese freshly milled salt and pepper**	*175 g/6 oz*

1. Put the potatoes into a casserole with 3 tbsp *(5 tbsp)* water. Cover and cook on high for about 5–6 minutes *(8–9 minutes)* or until very soft, stirring once or twice. Drain and mash until smooth.

2 Put the onion, leeks, celery, carrots and butter into a casserole. Cover and cook on high for about 7 minutes *(11–12 minutes)* or until cooked through.

3. Stir in the flour and mustard, then gradually add the milk. Stir in the peas or beans. Cook on HIGH for about 2½–3 minutes *(4½–5 minutes)*, stirring frequently, until the sauce comes to the boil and is thickened. Stir in two-thirds of the cheese and season to taste.

4. Spoon the mixture into a shallow flameproof dish. Top with the mashed potato and sprinkle the remaining cheese on top.

MICROWAVE + GRILL:
5. Stand the dish on a high rack. Cook on MEDIUM + GRILL for about 7 minutes *(9 minutes)* or until golden brown.

COMBINATION:
5. Preheat the oven to 200°C.

6. Put into the hot oven and cook on 200°C + MEDIUM for about 9 minutes *(14 minutes)* or until the top is golden brown.

PARSNIP AND CAERPHILLY BAKE

A delicious side dish for roast beef or lamb.

To serve 2		To serve 4
1 small	**onion, thinly sliced**	*1 medium*
1 tbsp	**butter**	*2 tbsp*
1 tbsp	**creamed horseradish sauce**	*2 tbsp*
150 ml/¼ pint	**single cream**	*300 ml/½ pint*
	freshly milled salt and pepper	
350 g/12 oz	**parsnips, thinly sliced**	*675 g/1½ lb*
55 g/2 oz	**grated Caerphilly cheese**	*115 g/4 oz*

1. Put the onion and butter into a casserole, cover and cook on HIGH for 3 minutes *(5 minutes)*.

2. Add the horseradish sauce, cream and seasoning to taste. Stir and cook on HIGH for about 1½ minutes *(2½ minutes)* until the mixture just comes to the boil.

3. Add the parsnips and stir well. Spoon evenly into a shallow flameproof dish.

MICROWAVE + GRILL:

4. Cover and cook on MEDIUM for about 10 minutes *(14 minutes)* or until just soft throughout. Sprinkle the cheese on top.

5. Stand on a high rack and cook on MEDIUM + GRILL for about 7 minutes *(9 minutes)* or until golden brown.

COMBINATION:

4. Cover and cook on 200°C + MEDIUM for about 10 minutes *(15 minutes)* or until just soft throughout. Sprinkle the cheese on top.

5. Uncover and cook on 200°C + MED-LOW for about 10 minutes *(15 minutes)* or until golden brown.

POTATO GRATIN WITH GARLIC HERBED CHEESE

Serve with lightly-cooked green beans and grilled tomatoes.

To serve 2		To serve 4
75 ml/2½ fl oz	**milk**	*150 ml/¼ pint*
125 g/4½ oz	**soft cheese with garlic and herbs**	*250 g/8 oz*
350 g/12 oz	**baking potatoes, very thinly sliced**	*675 g/1½ lb*
	freshly milled salt and pepper	

1. Put the milk and cheese into a bowl and cook on MED-HIGH for about 1 minute *(1½ minutes)*, stirring once, or until the cheese has melted and the mixture is smooth.

2. Arrange half the potato slices in a shallow flameproof dish. Season and pour over half the cheese mixture. Repeat with the remaining potato slices and cheese mixture.

MICROWAVE + GRILL:

3. Cover and cook on MEDIUM for 8–10 minutes *(12–15 minutes)*.

4. Remove cover, stand the dish on a high *(low)* rack and cook on GRILL + MED-LOW for about 8 minutes *(12 minutes)* or until the potatoes are soft throughout and the top is golden brown.

COMBINATION:

3. Preheat the oven to 220°C.

4. Cover and cook on 220°C + MEDIUM for 8–10 minutes *(12–15 minutes)*.

5. Remove cover and cook on 200°C + MED-LOW for about 10 minutes *(15 minutes)* or until the potatoes are soft throughout and the top is golden brown.

VEGETABLE-STUFFED PEPPERS

Delicious served freshly cooked with a jacket potato or cool to room temperature and serve with some hot garlic toast. Lightly toast thick slices of bread and generously spread the untoasted side with garlic butter – toast until golden.

To serve 2		*To serve 4*
1 tbsp	**olive oil**	*2 tbsp*
1 small	**onion, finely chopped**	*1 medium*
1 small	**aubergine, finely diced**	*1 medium*
175 g/6 oz	**courgettes, thinly sliced**	*250 g/9 oz*
3 tbsp	**dry white wine**	*6 tbsp*
4 tbsp	**tomato purée**	*8 tbsp*
	freshly milled salt and pepper	
2 large	**red or yellow peppers**	*4 large*

1. Put the oil and onion into a casserole. Cover and cook on HIGH for 1 minute *(2 minutes)*.

2. Stir in the aubergine, courgettes, wine and tomato purée. Cover and cook on HIGH for about 15 minutes *(20 minutes)*, stirring once or twice, or until very soft. Season with salt and pepper.

3. Preheat the oven to 200°C.

4. Cut the stem end off each pepper and remove the seeds and any pith. Stand the peppers in a small deep casserole or soufflé dish, of a size that will hold them upright. Fill the peppers with the vegetable mixture, pushing it in gently with a teaspoon. Replace the tops and add 2.5 cm/1 inch boiling water (from the kettle) to the dish.

5. Put into the hot oven and cook on 200°C + MEDIUM for about 14–15 minutes *(20–25 minutes)* or until the peppers are very soft when pierced with a fork.

BAKED TOMATOES

Excellent accompaniment to grilled or baked dishes.

To serve 2		To serve 4
2	**ripe beefsteak tomatoes**	4
25 g/1 oz	**butter**	55 g/2 oz
1	**garlic clove(s), crushed**	2
½	**finely grated rind of lemon**	1
1 tbsp	**finely chopped fresh parsley**	2 tbsp

1. Put the tomatoes into a bowl and cover with boiling water (from the kettle). Leave to stand for a few minutes – the skins will split. Drain and pull off the skins. Cut out the stem end. Place, stem-side down, in a shallow flameproof dish. Partly cut through each tomato two or three times.

2. Put the butter, garlic and lemon rind into a bowl. Cook on HIGH for 45 seconds *(1 minute)* or until melted and bubbling hot. Stir in the parsley. Spoon over the tomatoes.

3. Stand the dish on a high rack. Cook on MEDIUM + GRILL for about 6 minutes *(8 minutes)* or until piping hot and the tops are lightly browned.

POTATO GALETTE

Excellent served with grilled dishes or bean dishes This recipe is very good made with herb or garlic butter too.

To serve 2		To serve 4
25 g/1 oz	**butter**	*55 g/12 oz*
400 g/14 oz	**baking potatoes, peeled and very thinly sliced**	*675 g/1½ lb*
	freshly milled salt and pepper	
1 small	**onion**	*1 medium*
1 tsp	**caster sugar**	*2 tsp*

1. Put the butter into a small bowl and cook on HIGH for 20 seconds *(45 seconds)* or until melted.

2. Arrange the potato slices in a shallow flameproof dish, drizzling some of the butter and seasoning with salt and pepper between the layers. Thinly slice the onion, keeping the slices intact. Arrange the onion on top of the potato, drizzle over the remaining butter and sprinkle with the sugar.

MICROWAVE + GRILL:

3. Cover and cook on MED-HIGH for about 10 minutes *(15 minutes)*.
4. Uncover and stand the dish on a high *(low)* rack. Cook on MEDIUM + GRILL for about 6 minutes *(9 minutes)* or until the potatoes are very soft throughout and the top is golden brown.

COMBINATION:

3. Cover and cook on 200°C + MED-LOW for about 10 minutes *(15 minutes)*.

4. Uncover and cook on 200°C + MED-LOW for about 6 minutes *(10 minutes)* or until the potatoes are soft throughout and the top is golden brown.

SAUCY SPINACH

To serve 2		To serve 4
25 g/1 oz	**butter**	*55 g/2 oz*
25 g/1 oz	**fresh breadcrumbs**	*55 g/2 oz*
450 g/1 lb	**spinach, washed**	*900 g/2 lb*
1 tsp	**red wine vinegar**	*2 tsp*
	freshly milled salt and pepper	
150 ml/¼ pint	**milk**	*300 ml/½ pint*
1½ tbsp	**plain flour**	*3 tbsp*
55 g/2 oz	**grated mature Cheddar cheese**	*115 g/4 oz*
2	**medium eggs, separated**	*3*

1. Put the butter into a bowl and cook on HIGH for about 20 seconds *(45 seconds)* until melted. Add 2 tbsp *(4 tbsp)* to the breadcrumbs and mix with a fork until well combined.

2. Put the spinach into a casserole, cover and cook on HIGH for about 5½ minutes *(8 minutes)* until just soft. Drain thoroughly and finely chop. Stir in 1 tbsp *(2 tbsp)* of the melted butter, the vinegar and seasoning. Tip into a shallow ovenproof dish and level the top.

3. Into the remaining butter, whisk the milk and flour. Cook on HIGH for about 2 minutes *(3½ minutes)*, stirring frequently, until the sauce comes to the boil and is thickened and smooth. Beat in the cheese and egg yolks, then season to taste. Whisk the egg whites to soft peaks and, with a metal spoon, fold into the sauce. Spoon the mixture on top of the spinach and sprinkle with the buttered crumbs.

4. Preheat the oven to 200°C.

5. Put into the hot oven and cook on 200°C + MED-LOW for about 12–15 minutes *(18–20 minutes)* or until the topping is just firm and golden brown.

GARLIC AND HERB POTATO BAKE

A tasty way to serve potatoes – excellent with grilled meat, poultry or fish.

To serve 2		To serve 4
40 g/1½ oz	**butter**	*85 g/3 oz*
2	**garlic cloves, crushed**	*4*
1 tbsp	**finely chopped fresh parsley**	*2 tbsp*
2 tbsp	**finely chopped fresh chives**	*4 tbsp*
	freshly milled salt and pepper	
350 g/12 oz	**baking potatoes, peeled**	*675 g/1½ lb*

1. Lightly butter a shallow ovenproof dish and line the base with non-stick paper. Put the butter into a bowl and cook on HIGH for 1 minute *(1½ minutes)* or until melted. Stir in the garlic, parsley, chives and a good seasoning of salt and pepper.

2. Slice the potatoes thinly and arrange in layers in the dish, drizzling the butter mixture between each layer.

3. Cover and cook on 200°C + MED-LOW for about 10 minutes *(15 minutes)*.

4. Remove the cover and continue to cook on 200°C + MED-LOW for about 5–6 minutes *(8–10 minutes)* or until the potatoes are golden brown and cooked through.

5. Leave the dish to stand for a few minutes, then run a knife around the edge. Place a flat plate on top and invert to unmould the bake. Remove the paper. Place a warmed serving plate on top and turn the bake over again to bring the crisp top uppermost. Cut into wedges to serve.

CRUMB-TOPPED POTATO AND EMMENTHAL BAKE

Serve with grilled tomatoes and lightly cooked green beans.

To serve 2		To serve 4
450 g/1 lb	**baking potatoes, peeled**	*900 g/2 lb*
150 ml/¼ pint	**single cream**	*300 ml/½ pint*
2 tsp	**plain flour**	*1 tbsp*
pinch	**grated nutmeg**	*¼ tsp*
15 g/½ oz	**butter**	*25 g/1 oz*
	freshly milled salt and pepper	
115 g/4 oz	**grated Emmenthal cheese**	*225 g/8 oz*
25 g/1 oz	**fresh breadcrumbs**	*55 g/2 oz*

1. Cut the potatoes into 1 cm/½ inch dice. Put into a casserole and add 3 tbsp (*6 tbsp*) cold water. Cover and cook on HIGH for about 5 minutes (*8 minutes*), stirring once.

2. Put the cream into a bowl. Whisk in the flour and nutmeg, then add the butter. Cook on HIGH for about 2 minutes (*3 minutes*), whisking frequently, or until the sauce just comes to the boil and is thickened and smooth. Season to taste. Add three-quarters of the cheese and stir until melted.

3. Drain the potatoes and add to the sauce. Gently stir together. Spoon into a shallow flameproof dish. Combine the remaining cheese with the breadcrumbs and sprinkle over the top.

MICROWAVE + GRILL:

4. Stand on a high (*low*) rack. Cook on MED-LOW + GRILL for about 9–10 minutes (*14–15 minutes*) or until the potatoes are soft and the top golden brown.

COMBINATION:

4. Cook on 200°C + MED-LOW for about 18–20 minutes (*23–25 minutes*) or until the potatoes are soft and the top is golden brown.

LEEKS WITH HAM

A new twist to an old favourite.

To serve 2		To serve 4
25 g/1 oz	**garlic butter**	*55 g/2 oz*
40 g/1½ oz	**fresh breadcrumbs**	*85 g/3 oz*
4 small	**leeks**	*8 small*
75 ml/2½ fl oz	**vegetable stock**	*150 ml/¼ pint*
4	**cooked ham slices, or Quorn slices**	*8*
1 tsp	**Dijon mustard**	*1 tbsp*
75 ml/2½ fl oz	**double cream**	*150 ml/¼ pint*
	freshly milled salt and pepper	

1. Put the butter into a bowl and cook on HIGH for about 20 seconds *(45 seconds)* or until melted. Using a fork, mix in the breadcrumbs until evenly coated with the butter.

2. Put the leeks into a casserole (halve them if they are too long) and add the stock. Cover and cook on HIGH for about 5 minutes *(8 minutes)* or until just tender, rearranging them once.

3. Lay the ham or Quorn slices on the work surface and, lifting them with a fork, divide the leeks equally among them. Roll up and arrange in a shallow flameproof dish.

4. Add the mustard and cream to the pan juices. Cook on MED-HIGH for about 1 minute *(1½ minutes)*. Season to taste and pour over the leeks. Sprinkle the buttered crumbs over the top.

MICROWAVE + GRILL:

5. Stand on a high rack. Cook on MEDIUM + GRILL for about 5 minutes (7 *minutes*) or until golden brown.

COMBINATION:

5. Preheat the oven to 200°C. Put into the hot oven and cook on 200°C + MED-LOW for about 9–10 minutes *(10–12 minutes)* or until golden brown.

CARROT AND POTATO GRATIN

To serve 2		To serve 4
225 g/8 oz	baking potatoes, peeled and thinly sliced	450 g/1 lb
175 g/6 oz	carrots, thinly sliced	350 g/12 oz
	freshly milled salt and pepper	
55 g/2 oz	grated Emmenthal cheese	115 g/4 oz
1 tbsp	butter	2 tbsp
150 ml/¼ pint	hot vegetable stock	300 ml/½ pint

1. Arrange one-third of the vegetable slices in a greased shallow flameproof dish. Sprinkle with salt, pepper and half the cheese. Repeat the layers, ending with vegetables.

2. Stir the butter into the stock until melted. Pour over the vegetables.

MICROWAVE + GRILL:

3. Stand the dish on a high *(low)* rack. Cook on MEDIUM + GRILL for about 9–10 minutes *(13–15 minutes)* or until the vegetables are soft and the top is golden brown.

COMBINATION:

3. Preheat the oven to 200°C.

4. Cover and put into the hot oven. Cook on 200°C + MEDIUM for 9–10 minutes *(13–15 minutes)*. Uncover and continue cooking on 200°C + MEDIUM for about 8 minutes *(12 minutes)* until the vegetables are soft and the top is golden brown.

ROAST VEGETABLE PLATTER

Serves 2

1 large baking potato, scrubbed
2 small parsnips, peeled
2 carrots, peeled
2 small onions
1 tbsp olive oil
1 tbsp dried mixed herbs

1. Halve the potato lengthways and cut each half into four 'chips'. Leave the other vegetables whole or, if they are much larger than the potato pieces, halve them.

2. Pour the oil into a large food (freezer) bag and add the vegetables. Shake until they are well coated with oil. Add the herbs and shake again.

3. Tip the vegetables, in one layer, onto a flameproof plate.

MICROWAVE + GRILL:

4. Stand the plate on a high rack. Cook on MEDIUM + GRILL for about 8–10 minutes, turning the vegetables once, or until tender and golden.

COMBINATION:

4. Cook on 220°C + MEDIUM for about 12–15 minutes or until tender and golden.

MUSHROOM FLAN

Serves 4

280 g/10 oz mushrooms, sliced
20 cm/8 inch uncooked pastry case
2 medium eggs, lightly beaten
150 ml/¼ pint single cream
175 g/6 oz grated mature Cheddar cheese
55 g/2 oz frozen peas
Freshly milled salt and pepper

1. On the hob, quickly cook the mushrooms in a non-stick pan
   without fat, stirring, until golden brown. Brush the inside of the
   pastry case with a little of the beaten egg.

2. Preheat the oven to 220°C.

3. Put the empty pastry case into the hot oven and cook on 220°C +
   LOW for about 3–4 minutes until set.

4. Lightly beat together the eggs and cream. Stir in the cheese, peas
   and seasoning. Spoon the mushrooms into the pastry case and
   pour the egg mixture over the top.

5. Put into the hot oven and cook on 200°C + MED-LOW for about 20
   minutes or until the filling is set and golden brown.

STUFFED POTATOES

Baked jacket potatoes are always popular and so easy to make. The fillings use vegetarian options for bacon and sausages, but the choice is yours.

Each of the following suggestions fills one potato. Make the filling while you are cooking the potatoes (your cooker probably has an auto-cook program for the time and temperature). Halve the cooked potato horizontally and scoop out the flesh into a bowl. Continue as below.

CHEESE AND BACON FILLING

1 tbsp mayonnaise
1 tbsp sweetcorn relish
Freshly milled salt and pepper
1 vegetarian bacon rasher, crisply grilled and chopped
25 g/1 oz grated vegetarian hard cheese

1. Add the mayonnaise, relish and seasoning to the potato flesh and mash with a fork until smooth. Stir in the bacon and half the cheese.

2. Pile into the potato shells and top with the remaining cheese. Place the filled potatoes on a flameproof plate.

3. Preheat the grill.

4. Stand the plate on a high rack and cook on LOW + GRILL for 5–7½ minutes or until golden brown and piping hot.

PESTO AND PINE NUT FILLING

25 g/l oz butter
Freshly milled salt and pepper
1 tbsp green pesto
25 g/1 oz pine nuts
1 tbsp fruit chutney

1. Put the butter into a bowl and cook on HIGH for 20 seconds until melted. Add half to the potato flesh with seasoning to taste and mash with a fork until smooth. Stir in the pesto, pine nuts and chutney.

2. Pile into the potato shells and drizzle the remaining butter on top. Place the filled potatoes on a flameproof plate.

3. Preheat the grill.

4. Stand the plate on a high rack and cook on LOW + GRILL for 5–7½ minutes or until golden brown and piping hot.

SAUSAGE AND TOMATO FILLING

1 tbsp tomato purée or chutney
Freshly milled salt and pepper
1 cooked vegetarian sausage, thinly sliced
Soft butter

1. Add the tomato purée and seasoning to the potato flesh and mash with a fork until smooth. Stir in the sausage slices.

2. Pile into the potato shells and top with a small knob of butter. Place the filled potatoes on a flameproof plate.

3. Preheat the grill.

4. Stand the plate on a high rack and cook on LOW + GRILL for 5–7½ minutes or until golden brown and piping hot.

SPICED MAYONNAISE AND CHIVE FILLING

1 tbsp mayonnaise
1 tsp Chinese five-spice paste
Freshly milled salt and pepper
1 tbsp finely chopped fresh chives
55 g/2 oz grated vegetarian cheese
Soft butter

1. Add the mayonnaise, Chinese five-spice paste, seasoning and chives to the potato flesh and mash with a fork until smooth. Stir in the cheese.

2. Pile into the potato shells and top with a small knob of butter. Place the filled potatoes on a flameproof plate.

3. Preheat the grill.

4. Stand the plate on a high rack and cook on LOW + GRILL for 5–7½ minutes or until golden brown and piping hot.

4

PASTA, RICE AND PULSES

Our recipes use dried pasta and white rice (unless otherwise stated). If you prefer to use fresh pasta, remember it needs a very short cooking time – check the packet instructions and adjust cooking times to suit. Unless the recipe specifies otherwise, cook pasta and rice uncovered. Use a large bowl or casserole and hot liquid (use boiling water from the kettle). Pasta should be covered with boiling water by at least 5 cm/2 inches. Stirring occasionally prevents the pasta sticking together in clumps. Add a pinch of salt and a dash of oil if you wish, though we find it unnecessary. A standing time is important after cooking for the pasta to absorb water and soften. You can cover the bowl with a thick tea-towel to trap in the steam. Cooking rice is foolproof if you use the method where the rice grains absorb all the liquid to become plump and tender. Don't be surprised if you find that, at the end of the cooking time, not all the cooking liquid has been absorbed – just cover the bowl and leave the rice to stand for 5 minutes when it will finish cooking and absorb the liquid. Brown rice can be used in place of white in most of the recipes but you will need to increase both the amount of liquid used and the cooking time. Most brown rice needs about 750 ml/1¼ pints liquid to 115 g/4 oz rice and a cooking time of about 25 minutes. Ready-cooked beans, either canned or frozen, cook in just a few minutes.

LENTIL FISH PIE

m+g

Serves 4

450 g/1 lb skinless cod fillets
450 ml/16 fl oz milk
3 tbsp plain flour
½ tsp Dijon mustard
25 g/1 oz butter
Finely grated rind and juice of 1 lemon
115 g/4 oz grated Cheddar cheese
Freshly milled salt and pepper
50 g can anchovies
85 g/3 oz fresh bread, cubed
425 g can lentils, drained and rinsed
4 spring onions, finely chopped

1. Put the fish into a shallow casserole and pour over the milk. Cover and cook on HIGH for about 6 minutes or until just cooked. Lift the fish out onto a plate and flake, removing any bones. Tip the milk into a bowl and rinse out the casserole.

2. Into the milk, whisk the flour and mustard, then add the butter. Cook on HIGH for about 3–4 minutes, whisking frequently, or until the sauce comes to the boil and is thickened and smooth. Stir in 2 tsp lemon juice, the cheese and seasoning to taste. Stir in the cooked fish and spoon into the casserole. Cook on MED-HIGH for 3–4 minutes until bubbling hot.

3. Put the anchovies with their oil and the bread into a processor. Buzz to crumbs. Spoon over the top of the fish.

4. Preheat the grill.

5. Stand the casserole on a high rack and cook on MED-LOW + GRILL for 5–6 minutes or until golden brown.

6. Put the lentils, spring onions, lemon rind and remaining lemon juice into a casserole. Cover and cook on HIGH for 2–3 minutes, stirring once, until piping hot. Spoon around the edge of the casserole and serve.

TUNA AND MACARONI AU GRATIN

Delicious with a salad of sliced tomatoes and finely chopped spring onions, with a garlicky oil-and-vinegar dressing drizzled over the top.

To serve 2		To serve 4
115 g/4 oz	**macaroni**	*225 g/8 oz*
1 small	**onion, finely chopped**	*1 medium*
25 g/1 oz	**butter**	*55 g/2 oz*
25 g/1 oz	**plain flour**	*55 g/2 oz*
300 ml/½ pint	**milk**	*600 ml/1 pint*
	freshly milled salt and pepper	
2 tsp	**lemon juice**	*1 tbsp*
85 g/3 oz	**grated Cheddar cheese**	*140 g/5 oz*
227 g can	**tuna in brine, drained and flaked**	*two 227 g cans*

1. Put the macaroni into a bowl and cover generously with boiling water (from the kettle). Cook on HIGH for about 8 minutes *(9–10 minutes)*, stirring once. Cover and leave to stand.

2. Put the onion and butter into a bowl. Cook on HIGH for 1 minute *(1½ minutes)*. Stir in the flour and then the milk. Cook on HIGH for 3–4 minutes *(5–6 minutes),* whisking once or twice, or until the sauce comes to the boil and is smooth and thickened. Season to taste. Add the lemon juice and half the cheese, stirring until the cheese has melted, then add the tuna.

3. Drain the pasta well and stir into the cheese and tuna sauce. Spoon into a shallow flameproof dish and sprinkle the remaining cheese on top.

MICROWAVE + GRILL:
4. Stand the dish on a high *(low)* rack. Cook on MED-LOW + GRILL for about 8 minutes *(12 minutes)* or until golden brown.

COMBINATION:
4. Preheat the oven to 200°C.

5. Put the dish in the hot oven and cook on 200°C + MED-LOW for about 8 minutes *(12 minutes)* or until golden brown.

PASTA WITH CREAMY
BLUE CHEESE SAUCE

Serve this pasta dish with a salad of sliced ripe tomatoes and very thin rings of sweet red onion, sprinkled with salt, freshly milled black pepper and a pinch of sugar to bring out the flavour.

To serve 2		To serve 4
175 g/6 oz	**pasta shapes, such as shells**	350 g/12 oz
25 g/1 oz	**butter**	55 g/2 oz
55 g/2 oz	**fresh breadcrumbs**	115 g/4 oz
1 small	**onion, finely chopped**	1 medium
1 tsp	**plain flour**	2 tsp
1 tbsp	**finely chopped fresh thyme**	2 tbsp
150 ml/¼ pint	**milk**	300 ml/½ pint
150 ml/¼ pint	**hot vegetable stock**	300 ml/½ pint
115 g/4 oz	**mild blue cheese, diced**	225 g/8 oz
	freshly milled pepper	

1. Put the pasta in a bowl and cover generously with boiling water (from the kettle). Stir well. Cook on HIGH for 8 minutes *(10 minutes)*, stirring once. Cover and leave to stand.

2. Put the butter into a bowl and cook on HIGH for 20 seconds *(45 seconds)* until melted. Add half the butter to the breadcrumbs and toss lightly with a fork until combined.

3. Add the onion to the remaining butter. Cover and cook on HIGH for 2 minutes (3 *minutes)* until soft. Stir in the flour and thyme and cook on HIGH for 1 minute *(1½ minutes)*. Gradually stir in the milk, stock and cheese.

4. Cook on HIGH for 2½–4 minutes *(5–6 minutes)*, stirring once or twice, until the cheese has melted and the sauce is bubbling. Season with pepper.

5. Drain the pasta and add to the sauce. Stir gently until combined. Spoon into individual, or one large, shallow flameproof dish(es). Sprinkle the buttered crumbs on top.

MICROWAVE + GRILL:

6. Preheat the grill.

7. Stand the dish on a high *(low)* rack. Put under the hot grill and cook on LOW + GRILL for about 3½–4 minutes *(5½–6 minutes)* or until golden brown.

COMBINATION:

6. Preheat the oven to 200°C.

7. Put into the hot oven and cook on 200°C + LOW for about 7–8 minutes *(12 minutes)* until golden brown.

PASTA POTS

For vegetarians, omit the bacon and add a little more cheese.

To serve 2		To serve 4
115 g/4 oz	**pasta shapes or macaroni**	*225 g/8 oz*
25 g/1 oz	**butter**	*55 g/2 oz*
115 g/4 oz	**back bacon, chopped**	*225 g/8 oz*
1 medium	**onion, thinly sliced**	*1 large*
2 tbsp	**plain flour**	*4 tbsp*
300 ml/½ pint	**milk**	*600 ml/1 pint*
2 tsp	**dried mixed herbs**	*4 tsp*
85 g/3 oz	**grated mature Cheddar cheese**	*175 g/6 oz*
	freshly milled salt and pepper	
1	**tomato(es), sliced**	*2*

1. Put the pasta in a bowl and cover generously with boiling water (from the kettle). Stir well. Cook, uncovered, on HIGH for about 8 minutes *(10 minutes)*, stirring once or twice. Stir, cover and leave to stand.

2. Put the butter, bacon and onion in a casserole. Cover and cook on HIGH for 4–5 minutes *(6–7 minutes)*, stirring once or twice.

3. Blend in the flour and gradually stir in the milk, then the herbs. Cook on MED-HIGH for about 5 minutes *(8 minutes)*, stirring frequently, until the sauce comes to the boil and is thickened and smooth. Stir in half the cheese and season to taste.

4. Drain the pasta and stir into the sauce. Spoon into individual (or one) shallow flameproof dish(es). Top with the tomato slices and the remaining cheese.

MICROWAVE + GRILL:
5. Preheat the grill.

6. Stand the dish(es) on a high *(low)* rack and cook on MED-LOW + GRILL for 3–4 minutes *(5–6 minutes)* or until golden brown.

COMBINATION:
5. Preheat the oven to 220°C.

6. Put into the hot oven and cook on 220°C + LOW for about 10–12 minutes *(13–15 minutes)* or until golden brown.

BAKED PASTA WITH MUSHROOMS

To serve 2		To serve 4
115 g/4 oz	**penne pasta**	225 g/8 oz
175 ml/6 fl oz	**milk**	350 ml/12 fl oz
1½ tbsp	**plain flour**	3 tbsp
15 g/½ oz	**butter**	25 g/1 oz
2 tbsp	**grated Parmesan cheese**	4 tbsp
	freshly milled salt and pepper	
1 small	**onion, thinly sliced**	1 medium
1 tsp	**oil**	2 tsp
1	**garlic clove(s), crushed**	2
175 g/6 oz	**baby button mushrooms**	350 g/12 oz
227 g	**can chopped tomatoes**	400 g
55 g/2 oz	**grated Mozzarella cheese**	115 g/4 oz

1. Put the pasta into a bowl and cover generously with boiling water (from the kettle). Stir well. Cook on HIGH for 8 minutes *(12 minutes)*, stirring once or twice. Cover and leave to stand.

2. Put the milk into a bowl, whisk in the flour and add the butter. Cook for about 2 minutes *(3 minutes)*, whisking frequently, until the sauce comes to the boil and is thickened and smooth. Stir in the Parmesan cheese and season to taste.

3. Put the onion, oil and garlic into a casserole, cover and cook for 2 minutes *(3 minutes)* or until soft. Stir in the mushrooms and tomatoes. Cover and cook for 2 minutes *(3 minutes)*.

4. Drain the pasta. Add the mushroom mixture and stir lightly together. Tip into a shallow flameproof dish and pour the cheese sauce over. Sprinkle the Mozzarella cheese evenly on top.

MICROWAVE + GRILL:

5. Stand the dish on a high *(low)* rack. Cook on MEDIUM + GRILL for about 5–6 minutes *(8–10 minutes)* or until bubbling hot and golden brown.

COMBINATION:

5. Preheat the oven to 200°C.

6. Put into the hot oven and cook on 200°C + MED-LOW for about 9–10 minutes *(12–15 minutes)* or until bubbling hot and golden brown.

GNOCCHI WITH BOLOGNESE SAUCE

If time is short, instead of making polenta gnocchi, use one or two 400 g/14 oz packet(s) of potato gnocchi. Cook them, following packet instructions, after making the sauce.

To serve 2		To serve 4
115 g/4 oz	**instant polenta**	*225 g/8 oz*
	freshly milled salt and pepper	
15 g/½ oz	**butter**	*25 g/1 oz*
2 tsp	**olive oil**	*1 tbsp*
2	**streaky bacon rashers, finely chopped**	*4*
1 medium	**onion, finely chopped**	*1 large*
1 medium	**carrot, finely chopped**	*1 large*
2	**celery sticks, finely chopped**	*4*
1	**garlic clove(s), crushed**	*2*
225 g/8 oz	**extra lean minced beef**	*450 g/1 lb*
3 tbsp	**tomato purée**	*5 tbsp*
4 tbsp	**dry white vermouth**	*50 ml/2 fl oz*
½ tsp	**fennel seeds**	*1 tsp*
125 ml/4 fl oz	**hot beef stock**	*150 ml/¼ pint*
55 g/2 oz	**grated Mozzarella cheese**	*115 g/4 oz*

1. Put the polenta and a pinch of salt into a bowl. Gradually stir in 600 ml/1 pint *(1.2 litres/2 pints)* boiling water (from the kettle) to make a smooth mixture. Add the butter.

2. Cook on HIGH for about 5 minutes *(6–8 minutes)*, stirring occasionally, until the mixture is thick and leaves the side of the bowl. Spoon into a greased shallow container (such as a Swiss-roll tin), level the top and leave to stand until quite cold.

3. Meanwhile, make the Bolognese Sauce. Put the oil and bacon into a casserole. Cover and cook on HIGH for 2 minutes *(3 minutes)*. Stir in the vegetables and garlic, cover and cook on HIGH for 3 minutes *(5 minutes)*. Break up the mince with a fork and add to the casserole. Cook on HIGH for 3 minutes *(5 minutes)*, stirring once. Combine the tomato purée, vermouth, fennel seeds

and stock. Stir into the casserole. Cover and cook on HIGH for about 5 minutes (*8–9 minutes*). Uncover and cook on HIGH for about 4 minutes (*6 minutes*), stirring once, or until the sauce has thickened. Season to taste.

4. Turn out the gnocchi (polenta) and cut into small squares. Spoon the Bolognese sauce into the base of a shallow flameproof dish. Top with the gnocchi in overlapping rows. Sprinkle the cheese on top.

MICROWAVE + GRILL:

5. Stand on a high (*low*) rack. Cook on MED-LOW + GRILL for 10–12 minutes (*about 13–15 minutes*) or until bubbling hot and golden brown on top.

COMBINATION:

5. Heat the oven to 200°C.

6. Put into the hot oven and cook on 200°C + MED-LOW for about 14 minutes (*18–20 minutes*) until bubbling hot and the top is golden brown.

PASTA AND VEGETABLE GRATIN

To serve 2		To serve 4
175 g/6 oz	**pasta shapes**	*350 g/12 oz*
15 g/½ oz	**butter**	*25 g/1 oz*
2 small	**leeks, thinly sliced**	*3 medium*
2 small	**carrots, thinly sliced**	*4 small*
1	**garlic clove(s), crushed**	*2*
1 tbsp	**plain flour**	*2 tbsp*
300 ml/½ pint	**milk**	*600 ml/1 pint*
1	**vegetable stock cube(s), crumbled**	*2*
	freshly milled pepper	
115 g/4 oz	**grated Cheddar cheese**	*225 g/8 oz*
2	**tomatoes, sliced**	*4*

1. Put the pasta into a bowl and cover generously with boiling water (from the kettle). Cook on HIGH for 8 minutes *(12 minutes)*, stirring once or twice. Cover and leave to stand.

2. Put the butter, leeks, carrots and garlic into a casserole. Cover and cook on HIGH for 4½ minutes *(7½ minutes)*, stirring once, or until quite soft. Stir in the flour, then gradually add the milk. Add the stock cube(s). Cook on HIGH, stirring frequently, for about 4 minutes *(6 minutes)* or until the sauce comes to the boil and is thickened. Season with pepper. Add half the cheese and stir until melted.

3. Drain the pasta and add to the sauce and vegetables. Stir until combined, then tip into a flameproof dish. Arrange the tomato slices on top and sprinkle with the remaining cheese.

MICROWAVE + GRILL:
4. Stand the dish on a high *(low)* rack. Cook on GRILL + MED-LOW for about 5½ minutes *(9 minutes)* or until golden brown.

COMBINATION:
4. Preheat the oven to 200°C.

5. Cook on 200°C + MED-LOW for about 10–12 minutes *(16–18 minutes)* or until golden brown.

LAMB BIRYANI

Check the instructions on the packet – the rice may need rinsing before cooking. If wished, garnish this dish with sliced hard-boiled egg and/or crisp-fried onion rings. Good served with seasoned yogurt and mango chutney.

To serve 2		*To serve 4*
1 tsp	**oil**	*1 tbsp*
1 small	**onion, thinly sliced**	*1 medium*
1	**garlic clove(s), crushed**	*2*
1 tsp	**chilli sauce**	*2 tsp*
1 tsp	**ground coriander**	*2 tsp*
½ tsp	**ground cumin**	*1 tsp*
½ tsp	**ground turmeric**	*1 tsp*
175 g/6 oz	**lean lamb, thinly sliced**	*350 g/12 oz*
115 g/4 oz	**basmati rice**	*225 g/8 oz*
227 g can	**chopped tomatoes**	*400 g can*
250 ml/9 fl oz	**hot vegetable or lamb stock**	*400 ml/14 fl oz*
	freshly milled salt and pepper	

1. Put the oil, onion, garlic, chilli sauce and spices into an ovenproof casserole, cover and cook on HIGH for 2 minutes *(3 minutes)*.

2. Stir in the lamb, cover and cook on 200°C + HIGH for 3 minutes *(5 minutes)*.

3. Add the rice, tomatoes, hot stock and seasoning. Stir well. Cover and cook on 200°C + MEDIUM for about 10 minutes *(15 minutes)*, stirring once or twice, until the rice and lamb are tender and almost all the liquid has been absorbed. Leave to stand, covered, for 5 minutes then fluff with a fork and serve.

STUFFED PASTA AU GRATIN

While the sauce is cooking, put together a salad of juicy orange segments and peppery watercress, sprinkle with a little oil-and-vinegar dressing, pile into individual salad bowls and top with crunchy croûtons.

To serve 2		To serve 4
25 g/1 oz	**butter**	*55 g/2 oz*
55 g/2 oz	**fresh breadcrumbs**	*115 g/4 oz*
2 tbsp	**freshly grated Parmesan cheese**	*4 tbsp*
225 g/8 oz	**filled fresh pasta such as tortellini or cappelletti**	*450 g/1 lb*
1 tsp	**oil**	*2 tsp*
1 small	**onion, thinly sliced**	*1 medium*
1	**garlic clove(s), crushed**	*2*
227 g	**can chopped tomatoes**	*400 g*
1 tsp	**finely chopped fresh or dried herbs**	*2 tsp*
2 tsp	**red wine vinegar**	*1 tbsp*
2 tsp	**sugar**	*1 tbsp*
	freshly milled salt and pepper	

1. Put the butter in a bowl and cook on HIGH for 20 seconds *(45 seconds)* until melted. Using a fork, mix in the breadcrumbs and cheese until evenly combined.

2. Put the pasta in a bowl and cover with boiling water (from the kettle). Stir well. Cook on HIGH for about 8 minutes *(12 minutes)*, stirring once or twice. Cover and leave to stand.

3. Put the oil, onion and garlic into a casserole, cover and cook on HIGH for 2½ minutes *(4½ minutes)*. Stir in the tomatoes, herbs, vinegar, sugar and seasoning. Cover and cook on HIGH for 5½ minutes *(9–10 minutes)*, stirring once or twice.

4. Drain the pasta and tip into a shallow flameproof dish. Spoon the sauce over and top with the buttered crumbs, making sure all the pasta is covered.

MICROWAVE + GRILL:

5. Preheat the grill.

6. Stand the dish on a high *(low)* rack. Put under the hot grill and cook on LOW + GRILL for about 6 minutes *(9 minutes)* until golden brown.

COMBINATION:

5. Preheat the oven to 200°C.

6. Put into the hot oven and cook on 200°C + LOW for about 10 minutes *(15 minutes)* until golden brown.

SMOKED FISH LASAGNE

$$\boxed{\text{C}}$$

This lasagne can be made in advance, covered and refrigerated for several hours or overnight before baking. Leave the cooked lasagne to stand for 5 minutes before cutting into portions and it will be much easier to serve.

A simple green salad would go well with this dish.

Serves 4

375 g/13 oz smoked haddock
2 smoked back bacon rashers, finely chopped
1 medium leek, thinly sliced
115 g/4 oz button mushrooms, sliced
600 ml/1 pint milk
3 tbsp plain flour
25 g/1 oz butter
Freshly milled salt and pepper
4 tbsp whipping cream
9 sheets no-cook lasagne verdi
2 tomatoes, thinly sliced
4 tbsp grated Parmesan cheese

1. Lay the fish in a shallow dish and just cover with water. Cover and cook on MED-HIGH for 5–6 minutes or until just cooked through. Drain, then flake, discarding skin and bones.

2. Put the bacon and leek into a medium casserole, cover and cook on HIGH for 2½–3 minutes. Stir in the mushrooms, cover and cook on HIGH for 1½–2 minutes.

3. Put the milk into a bowl. Whisk in the flour then add the butter. Cook on HIGH for about 5–6 minutes, stirring frequently, or until the sauce comes to the boil and is thickened and smooth. Season to taste.

4. Add half the sauce to the mushrooms and leeks. Add the fish and gently stir together. Add the cream to the remaining sauce and beat until smooth.

5. Spoon a thin layer of the cream sauce into a shallow rectangular

ovenproof dish. Top with a layer of pasta, fish and a final layer of pasta. Pour over the remaining cream sauce, making sure the pasta is completely covered. Arrange the tomatoes on top and sprinkle with the cheese.

6. Cook on 200°C + MED-LOW for about 25–30 minutes until the pasta is cooked throughout and the top is golden brown.

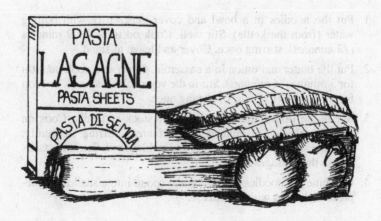

SAUSAGE AND VEGETABLE HOTPOT

To serve 2		To serve 4
115 g/4 oz	noodles	175 g/6 oz
15 g/½ oz	butter	25 g/1 oz
1 medium	onion, thinly sliced	1 large
115 g/4 oz	frozen mixed vegetables	225 g/8 oz
1½ tbsp	plain flour	3 tbsp
150 ml/¼ pint	hot vegetable or chicken stock	300 ml/½ pint
75 ml/2½ fl oz	milk	150 ml/¼ pint
	freshly milled salt and pepper	
225 g/8 oz	frankfurter sausages, thickly sliced	450 g/1 lb
25 g/1 oz	grated Cheddar cheese	55 g/2 oz

1. Put the noodles in a bowl and cover generously with boiling water (from the kettle). Stir well. Cook on HIGH for 9 minutes *(12 minutes)*, stirring once. Cover and leave to stand.

2. Put the butter and onion in a casserole. Cover and cook on HIGH for 3 minutes *(5 minutes)*. Stir in the vegetables and cook on HIGH for 4 minutes *(6 minutes)*, stirring once.

3. Stir in the flour. Gradually stir in the stock and milk. Cook on HIGH for about 3–4 minutes *(5–6 minutes)*, stirring frequently, until the sauce comes to the boil and is thickened. Season to taste. Stir in the sausages.

4. Combine the noodles and sauce and spoon into a shallow flame-proof dish. Top with the cheese.

MICROWAVE + GRILL:

5. Preheat the grill.

6. Stand the dish on a high *(low)* rack. Put under the hot grill and cook on LOW + GRILL for about 5 minutes *(7–8 minutes)* until golden brown.

COMBINATION:

5. Preheat the oven to 200°C.

6. Put into the hot oven and cook on 200°C + LOW for about 6 minutes *(8–9 minutes)* until golden brown.

5

FISH AND SHELLFISH

Cooking fish by microwave-only function is similar to poaching or steaming it conventionally, retaining all the freshness and texture without the fish becoming dry. Cooking fish on microwave + grill or on combination is just as successful, plus you can crisp and brown the skin or the top of the dish, as in Seafood Pie or Trout with a Mustard Glaze.

The cooking time for each method depends on the thickness of the fish and whether it is whole or in fillets. For best results, use the grill or a high temperature, with a low microwave setting. Always slash the skin of whole fish to prevent it bursting and, before cooking, lightly brush with oil or melted butter.

SALMON AND POTATO LAYER

A lightly-cooked vegetable, such as broccoli, green beans or finely shredded Savoy cabbage, would go well with this dish.

To serve 2		To serve 4
350 g/12 oz	**new potatoes, scrubbed**	*675 g/1½ lb*
225 g/8 oz	**skinless salmon fillet**	*450 g/1 lb*
150 ml/¼ pint plus extra	**milk**	*300 ml/½ pint plus extra*
1½ tbsp	**plain flour**	*3 tbsp*
pinch	**mustard powder**	*¼ tsp*
15 g/½ oz	**butter**	*25 g/1 oz*
	freshly milled salt and pepper	
55 g/2 oz	**grated Cheddar cheese**	*115 g/4 oz*
half a 50 g can	**anchovies, drained**	*50 g can*

1. Put the potatoes into a casserole with 3 tbsp (*6 tbsp*) water. Cover and cook on HIGH for about 7–8 minutes (*10–12 minutes*) or until just tender. Leave to stand.

2. Put the fish and milk into a casserole. Cover and cook on HIGH for about 4 minutes (*6 minutes*) or until the fish flakes easily. Remove the fish to a plate and flake.

3. Tip the milk into a measuring jug and make up to 150 ml/¼ pint (*300 ml/½ pint*) with extra milk if necessary. Whisk in the flour and mustard, then add the butter. Cook on HIGH for about 3 minutes (*4 minutes*), whisking frequently, or until the sauce comes to the boil and is thickened and smooth. Season to taste. Stir in the fish and half the cheese.

4. Drain the potatoes and cut into slices. Layer half in a shallow flameproof dish. Spoon over the fish and sauce and top with the remaining potatoes. Arrange the anchovies on top and sprinkle with the cheese.

MICROWAVE + GRILL:

5. Stand the dish on a high *(low)* rack.

6. Cook on MED-LOW + GRILL for about 6 minutes *(8–9 minutes)* or until golden brown.

COMBINATION:

5. Preheat the oven to 200°C.

6. Put into the hot oven and cook on 200°C + MED-LOW for about 9–10 minutes *(13–15 minutes)* or until golden brown.

TROUT WITH MUSTARD GLAZE

Hot new potatoes go well with this rich-tasting fish dish.

Serves 2

1 tbsp oil
1 tbsp clear honey
1 tbsp Dijon mustard
1 medium lemon
2 trout, about 225 g/8 oz each, thawed if frozen

1. Whisk together the oil, honey and mustard. Finely grate the rind and squeeze the juice from half the lemon and whisk in.

2. Brush the trout, inside and out, with the oil mixture and lay them, head to tail on an ovenproof plate. Drizzle any remaining mixture over the top. Slice the remaining lemon half and arrange the slices in the trout cavities.

MICROWAVE + GRILL:

3. Stand on a high rack. Cook on LOW + GRILL for 10–12 minutes, turning once, or until the fish is cooked through and the skin is crisp.

COMBINATION:

3. Preheat the oven to 250°C.

4. Cook on 250°C + LOW for 10–12 minutes or until the fish is cooked through and the skin is crisp.

TUNA AND SWEETCORN FLAN

Serves 4

225 g/8 oz shortcrust pastry
3 medium eggs, lightly beaten
425 g can creamed sweetcorn
227 g can tuna in brine, drained and flaked
6 spring onions, sliced
Freshly milled salt and pepper

1. Roll out the pastry and use to line a 20 cm/8 inch flan dish. Brush the inside of the pastry case with some of the beaten egg, then chill for 30 minutes.

2. Meanwhile, preheat the oven to 220°C.

3. Lightly whisk the sweetcorn into the eggs. Stir in the tuna, onions and seasoning.

4. Put the empty flan case into the hot oven and cook on 220°C + LOW for about 4 minutes until set.

5. Pour the sweetcorn mixture into the flan case. Put into the hot oven and cook on 220°C + MED-LOW for about 17–20 minutes until set and golden brown.

FISH FILLETS WITH SOURED CREAM AND CAPER TOPPING

To serve 2		To serve 4
1 tbsp	plain flour	2 tbsp
	salt and freshly milled pepper	
225 g/8 oz	white fish fillets or steaks	450 g/1 lb
5 tbsp	soured cream	150 ml/¼ pint
5 tbsp	mayonnaise	150 ml/¼ pint
2	spring onions, thinly sliced	4
1 tsp	lemon juice	2 tsp
1 tbsp	capers, finely chopped	2 tbsp
25 g/1 oz	grated Cheddar cheese	55 g/2 oz

1. Combine the flour with a generous seasoning of salt and pepper. Use to coat the fish on both sides. Place the fish in a single layer in a lightly buttered flameproof dish.

2. Combine the soured cream, mayonnaise, onions, lemon juice and capers. Spoon over the fish, making sure it is completely covered. Sprinkle the cheese on top of the sauce.

MICROWAVE + GRILL:

3. Preheat the grill.

4. Stand the dish on a high *(low)* rack. Put under the hot grill and cook on MED-HIGH + GRILL for about 5–6 minutes *(8–9 minutes)* or until the fish is cooked and the top is golden brown.

COMBINATION:

3. Preheat the oven to 180°C.

4. Put into the hot oven and cook on 180°C + MEDIUM for about 14–15 minutes *(18–20 minutes)* or until the fish is cooked and the top is golden brown.

SALMON AND CHEESE BAKE

This creamy soufflé-like casserole goes well with lightly-cooked green beans or asparagus spears – serve them hot with a little herbed oil-and-vinegar salad dressing instead of butter.

To serve 2		To serve 4
25 g/1 oz	**butter, melted**	*55 g/2 oz*
100 g/3½ oz	**cooked, skinless salmon fillet**	*200 g/7 oz*
3 (about 85 g/ 3 oz total)	**fresh white bread slices, cubed**	*6 (about 175g/ 6 oz total)*
55 g/2 oz	**grated Emmenthal cheese**	*115 g/4 oz*
2 tbsp	**finely chopped fresh tarragon or chives**	*3 tbsp*
2 small	**eggs**	*3 medium*
300 ml/½ pint	**milk**	*600 ml/1 pint*
	freshly milled salt and pepper	

1. Generously brush the inside of a casserole with some of the butter. Remove any bones from the salmon and flake into small pieces. Combine the salmon, bread, cheese and herb. Tip the mixture into the casserole.

2. Whisk together the eggs, milk and seasoning. Strain over the casserole. Drizzle the remaining butter over the top.

3. Preheat the oven to 200°C.

4. Uncover the casserole and put into the hot oven. Cook on 200°C + MEDIUM for about 18–20 minutes *(28–30 minutes)* or until puffed and golden brown. Serve immediately.

BAKED FISH WITH ORANGE AND SPRING ONION SAUCE

Serves 2

1 medium orange
2 whole fish (trout, snapper, tilapia), 280–350 g/10–12 oz each
40 g/1½ oz butter
2 tsp clear honey
4 spring onions, finely sliced
2 tsp light soy sauce
1 tsp cornflour
50 ml/2 fl oz fish or vegetable stock
Freshly milled salt and pepper

1. With a vegetable peeler, pare the thin zest from the orange and cut into thin strips. Squeeze the juice.

2. With a sharp knife, make a few cuts in the skin on both sides of each fish.

3. Put the butter and honey in a small bowl and cook on HIGH for about 25 seconds or until melted. Stir in the onions and soy sauce. Brush the mixture over the fish, inside and outside, and lay them, head to tail, on a large flameproof plate. Drizzle any remaining butter mixture on top.

MICROWAVE + GRILL:

4. Preheat the grill.

5. Put the dish on a high rack and cook on LOW + GRILL for about 4–5 minutes each side until golden and cooked through.

6. Lift the fish, reserving the juices, onto a warm plate and keep warm.

7. In a bowl or jug, whisk the cornflour into the orange juice. Stir in the stock, orange zest and the reserved juices. Cook on HIGH for about 2 minutes, stirring once or twice, or until the sauce comes to boil and is thickened. Season to taste, pour over the fish and serve.

COMBINATION:

4. Preheat the oven to 220°C.

5. Put the dish on a low rack and cook on 220°C + LOW for about 12–15 minutes, turning them once, until cooked through.

6. Lift the fish, reserving the juices, onto a warm plate and keep warm.

7. In a bowl or jug, whisk the cornflour into the orange juice. Stir in the stock, orange zest and the reserved juices. Cook on HIGH for about 2 minutes, stirring once or twice, or until the sauce comes to the boil and is thickened. Season to taste, pour over the fish and serve.

SMOKED HADDOCK AU GRATIN

Good with some grilled tomatoes. Put halved tomatoes on the plate alongside the fish, topping each half with a pinch of sugar. Grill them with the fish.

To serve 2		To serve 4
280 g/10 oz	**smoked haddock**	*550 g/1¼ lb*
half quantity	**Cheese Rarebit (page 40)**	*full quantity*

1. Cut the fish into two *(four)* portions and place on a flameproof dish. Slice the Rarebit and arrange on top of the fish.

2. Stand the dish on a high *(low)* rack. Cook on MEDIUM + GRILL for about 8 minutes *(12 minutes)* or until the fish is cooked and the top is golden brown.

SEAFOOD PIE

Just serve with peas or carrots, tossed with butter and finely chopped fresh parsley.

Serves 4

675 g/1½ lb potatoes, peeled and diced
450 ml/16 fl oz milk
225 g/8 oz skinless smoked fish such as haddock, trout or cod
225 g/8 oz skinless white fish such as haddock or salmon
25 g/1 oz flour
Pinch of cayenne pepper
85 g/3 oz butter
Freshly milled salt and pepper
6 spring onions, sliced
175 g/6 oz frozen mixed shellfish, mussels, cockles, prawns

1. Put the potatoes and 4 tbsp milk into a casserole. Cover and cook on HIGH for about 9–10 minutes, stirring once or twice, until quite soft.

2. Meanwhile, cut the fish into bite-sized pieces, discarding any bones.

3. Put the remaining milk into a bowl. Whisk in the flour and cayenne, then add 55 g/2 oz butter. Cook on HIGH for about 5 minutes, whisking frequently, until the sauce comes to the boil and is thickened and smooth. Season to taste. Stir in the fish, onions and shellfish. Cook on HIGH for 3–4 minutes, stirring once.

4. Mash the potatoes and add salt and pepper. Tip the fish mixture into a shallow ovenproof dish and spoon the potatoes on top. Melt the remaining butter and drizzle over the top.

MICROWAVE + GRILL:

5. Stand the dish on a low rack. Cook on MED-LOW + GRILL for 10–15 minutes or until bubbling hot and golden brown.

COMBINATION:

5. Preheat the oven to 200°C.

6. Put into the hot oven and cook on 200°C + MED-LOW for about 12–15 minutes until bubbling hot and golden brown.

COD WITH BACON AND CHEESE

Delicious with mashed potatoes.

The Cheese Rarebit mixture thickens when chilled. To use it, cut into slices – it softens and spreads during cooking.

To serve 2		To serve 4
2	**back bacon rashers**	*4*
280 g/10 oz	**thick cod fillets**	*550 g/1¼ lb*
half quantity	**Cheese Rarebit (page 40)**	*full quantity*

1. Grill or fry the bacon until cooked. Cut the fish into two (four) portions and place in a flameproof dish. Place the bacon on top. Slice the Rarebit and arrange on top.

2. Stand the dish on a high *(low)* rack. Cook on MED-HIGH + GRILL for about 6 minutes *(10 minutes)* or until the fish is cooked and the top is golden brown.

FISH FLORENTINE

Good with buttered new potatoes or creamy mashed potatoes.

To serve 2		To serve 4
225 g/8 oz	cook-in-the-bag fresh spinach	450 g/1 lb
	freshly milled salt and pepper	
2	skinless white fish fillets, about 175 g/6 oz each	4
150 ml/¼ pint	milk	300 ml/½ pint
1 tbsp	plain flour	2 tbsp
15 g/½ oz	butter	25 g/1 oz
55 g/2 oz	grated Mozzarella cheese	115 g/4 oz
half a 50g can	anchovy fillets, drained	50 g can

1. Cook the spinach following packet instructions. Drain well, then roughly chop. Put into a shallow flameproof dish.

2. Season the fish. Lightly roll up, skinned-side inside, and arrange on top of the spinach.

3. Put the milk into a bowl. Whisk in the flour, then add the butter. Cook on HIGH for about 3 minutes *(4 minutes)*, whisking frequently, or until the sauce just comes to the boil and is thickened and smooth. Stir in the cheese and season to taste. Spoon over the fish and top with the anchovy fillets.

MICROWAVE + GRILL:

4. Stand the dish on a high *(low)* rack. Cook on MEDIUM + GRILL for about 8–10 minutes *(12–15 minutes)* or until the fish is cooked and the top is golden brown.

COMBINATION:

4. Preheat the oven to 200°C.

5. Put into the hot oven and cook on 200°C + MEDIUM for about 8–10 minutes *(12–15 minutes)* or until the fish is cooked and the top is golden brown.

FISH PARCELS

Serve each parcel unopened – so that each person can enjoy the delicious aroma. Add some hot buttered rice or baby new potatoes.

To serve 2		To serve 4
½	**finely grated rind and juice of lemon**	*1*
1 tbsp	**olive oil**	*2 tbsp*
1 tbsp	**sweet chilli sauce**	*2 tbsp*
2	**thick cod or salmon cutlets, skinned**	*4*
1 medium	**tomato(es)**	*2 medium*
1 medium	**onion, thinly sliced**	*1 large*
	freshly milled salt and pepper	

1. Put the lemon rind, juice, oil and chilli sauce into a bowl and whisk until combined. Put the fish into a shallow non-metallic dish and pour over the lemon mixture. Turn the fish to coat it with the marinade on all sides. Cover and chill for 1–2 hours.

2. Put the tomato(es) into a bowl and cover with boiling water (from the kettle). Leave until the skins begin to split – they will then slip off easily. Cut out the stem end and roughly chop the flesh.

3. Put the onion into a casserole. Carefully drain the marinade from the fish into the casserole. Cover and cook for 3 minutes, stirring once, until soft. Stir in the tomato(es).

4. Preheat the oven to 180°C.

5. Cut two *(four)* squares of greaseproof paper, each large enough to generously wrap the fish. Place a fish portion in the centre of each square and spoon the vegetables on top. Fold the paper to make a neat parcel, tucking the open ends underneath. Place the parcels on a flat plate.

6. Put into the hot oven and cook on 180°C + MED-LOW for about 10 minutes *(12–15 minutes)* or until the fish is just opaque.

7. Serve piping hot.

TUNA AND
POTATO BAKE

Sliced tomatoes and coleslaw would go well with this dish.

To serve 2		To serve 4
1	**garlic clove(s), crushed**	*2*
150 ml/¼ pint	**milk**	*300 ml/½ pint*
2 tsp	**plain flour**	*1 tbsp*
15 g/12 oz	**butter**	*25 g/1 oz*
	freshly milled salt and pepper	
350 g/12 oz	**baking potatoes, peeled**	*675 g/1½ lb*
185 g	**can(s) tuna, drained and flaked**	*Two 185 g*
55 g/2 oz	**grated Edam cheese**	*115 g/4 oz*

1. Put the garlic and milk into a bowl. Whisk in the flour, then add the butter. Cook on HIGH for about 4 minutes *(6 minutes),* whisking frequently, until the sauce comes to the boil and is thickened and smooth. Season to taste.

2. Cut the potatoes into 1 cm/¹/₂ inch cubes and add to the sauce with the tuna. Spoon the mixture into a shallow, lightly-buttered flameproof dish.

MICROWAVE + GRILL:

3. Cover and cook on MEDIUM for 5 minutes *(8 minutes).*

4. Sprinkle the cheese on top. Stand the dish on a high *(low)* rack and cook on MEDIUM + GRILL for about 6 minutes *(9 minutes)* until the potatoes are soft throughout and golden brown on top.

COMBINATION:

3. Sprinkle the cheese on top. Cook on 220°C + MED-LOW for about 18–20 minutes *(26–30 minutes)* or until the potatoes are soft throughout and the top is golden brown.

6

MEAT

The versatility of a combination cooker is used to the full in these recipes. Soften the vegetables or make a sauce on microwave setting, add the other ingredients and then continue cooking on combination for a tender, melt-in-the-mouth result – and in much less time than a conventionally-cooked version. Stirring food during cooking will ensure an even result in some dishes.

In some recipes which use microwave + grill, we recommend using a high rack for two-portion dishes and a low rack for four, to ensure that food in the larger dishes is fully cooked or heated without the top becoming too brown. The first time you make a dish, keep an eye on it – some grills brown quicker than others.

BEEF AND PEPPER STRUDEL

C

Serve piping hot with a crisp green salad.

Serves 4

1 tsp oil
1 medium onion, thinly sliced
1 medium red pepper, stalk and seeds removed and thinly sliced
1 garlic clove, crushed
375 g/13 oz extra-lean minced beef
1 tsp fennel seeds or mixed dried herbs
2 tbsp tomato purée
225 g/8 oz puff pastry
115 g/4 oz Gouda cheese, diced
1 small egg, beaten
Sesame or poppy seeds

1. Put the oil, onion, pepper and garlic into a casserole. Cover and cook on HIGH for 3 minutes. Break up the mince with a fork and add to the vegetables.

2. Cover and cook for about 5 minutes, stirring once, until the meat is no longer pink. Stir in the seeds or herbs and tomato purée. Cook, uncovered, on HIGH for 5 minutes, stirring once. Leave to cool.

3. Preheat the oven to 200°C.

4. Roll out the pastry to 35 x 25 cm/14 x 10 inches and trim the edges. Sprinkle the cheese down the centre and top with the meat. Dampen the pastry edges. To enclose the filling, fold the shorter edges over 2.5 cm/1 inch, then fold the longer edges over, overlapping them by 2.5 cm/1 inch.

5. Place the pastry roll, seam-side down, on a dampened flat ovenproof plate. Using a very sharp knife, slash across the top of the pastry in several places. Brush with beaten egg and sprinkle with seeds.

6. Put into the hot oven and cook at 200°C + MEDIUM for about 15 minutes until golden brown.

SPICED BEEF WITH CRANBERRIES

Lots of delicious sauce in this dish. Serve it with mashed potatoes, beans or rice.

Serves 4–6

1 tsp oil
1 large onion, thinly sliced
1 tsp sugar
1 tsp ground cinnamon
½ tsp ground cloves
1 tsp ground ginger
900 g/2 lb lean braising steak, cut into bit-sized pieces
300 ml/½ pint beef stock
3 tbsp red wine vinegar
1 tbsp cornflour
190 g jar cranberry sauce
Freshly milled salt and pepper
Finely chopped fresh parsley

1. Put the oil and onion into a casserole, cover and cook on HIGH for 3 minutes, stirring once.

2. Stir in the sugar and spices. Cover and cook on HIGH for 1 minute.

3. Add the meat, stock and vinegar. Stir well.

4. Cover and cook on 160°C + HIGH for 5 minutes. Stir well.

5. Cover and cook on 160°C + MED-LOW for about 38–50 minutes, stirring occasionally, or until the meat is tender. Stir the cornflour into 1 tbsp cold water until smooth and stir into the casserole.

6. Stir in the cranberry sauce. Cover and continue to cook on 160°C + MED-LOW for 10 minutes.

7. Season to taste and serve sprinkled with chopped parsley.

STUFFED SQUASH

Acorn squash, with hard (inedible) orange and green skins, make perfect containers for this tasty filling of minced beef and garlicky cheese. Just add some hot garlic bread and a crisp green salad for a quick meal.

To serve 2		To serve 4
1	large acorn squash	2
1 small	onion, finely chopped	1 medium
2	celery sticks, finely chopped	4
1 tsp	oil	2 tsp
175 g/6 oz	extra lean minced beef	350 g/12 oz
1 tbsp	tomato purée	2 tbsp
50 g/1¾ oz	soft cheese with herbs and garlic	100 g/3½ oz
	freshly milled salt and pepper	
25 g/1 oz	smoked hard cheese, thinly sliced	55 g/2 oz

1. Cut the squash in half horizontally. Scoop out and discard all the seeds and pith.

2. Put the onion, celery and oil in a medium casserole. Cover and cook on HIGH for about 3 minutes (*5 minutes*) until soft, stirring once. Using a fork, break up the meat and add to the casserole with the tomato purée.

3. Cover and cook on HIGH for about 5 minutes (*8 minutes*), stirring once, until the meat is no longer pink.

4. Gradually stir in the soft cheese and seasoning. Place the squash in a shallow flameproof dish and fill with the meat mixture.

MICROWAVE + GRILL:

5. Cover and cook on MEDIUM for about 15 minutes (*20–23 minutes*) until the flesh of the squash is soft.

6. Top with the sliced cheese. Put on a high *(low)* rack. Cook on
   MEDIUM + GRILL for about 5 minutes *(8 minutes)* until golden
   brown.

COMBINATION:

5. Cover and cook on 200°C + MEDIUM for about 15 minutes *(20–23
   minutes)* until the flesh of the squash is soft.

6. Top with the sliced cheese and continue to cook on 200°C +
   MEDIUM for about 4 minutes *(6 minutes)* until golden brown.

POTATO-TOPPED BEEF AND WINE CASSEROLE

The meat base may be cooked in advance (steps 1–4). Before continuing with the recipe, cook the meat mixture, covered, on HIGH for 5–8 minutes, stirring occasionally, until it comes to the boil.

Serve with lightly-cooked carrots, tossed with melted butter and finely chopped fresh parsley.

Serves 4

3 tbsp plain flour
2 tbsp dried mixed herbs
675 g/1½ lb lean braising steak, cubed
115 g/4 oz streaky bacon, chopped
1 medium onion, thinly sliced
2 garlic cloves, crushed
400 ml/14 fl oz dry red wine
2 tsp brown sugar
Freshly milled salt and pepper
450 g/1 lb peeled potatoes
4 tbsp milk
25 g/1 oz butter
1 medium egg, separated
55 g/2 oz grated Cheddar cheese

1. Combine the flour and herbs in a food (freezer) bag and add the steak. Secure the opening and shake well to coat the meat with the flour.

2. Put the bacon, onion and garlic into an ovenproof casserole. Cover and cook on HIGH for 4 minutes, stirring once.

3. Add the meat with any remaining flour, the wine and sugar. Stir well.

MICROWAVE + GRILL:

4. Cover and cook on HIGH for 5 minutes. Stir well, cover and cook on MED-LOW for about 50–60 minutes, stirring once or twice, or until the steak is just tender. Season to taste.

5. Meanwhile, boil the potatoes (on the hob) until soft, then drain and mash. Add the milk, butter, egg yolk, salt and pepper. Beat until the butter has melted. Beat in half the cheese. Whisk the egg white until stiff, then fold into the potato mixture. Spoon the potato mixture on top of the casserole and sprinkle with the remaining cheese.

6. Stand the dish on a rack and cook on MED-LOW + GRILL for about 10 minutes until golden brown.

COMBINATION:

4. Cover and cook on 160°C + HIGH for 5 minutes. Stir well, cover and cook on 160°C + MED-LOW for about 1 hour, stirring once or twice, or until the steak is just tender. Season to taste.

5. Meanwhile, boil the potatoes (on the hob) until soft, then drain and mash. Add the milk, butter, egg yolk, salt and pepper. Beat until the butter has melted. Beat in half the cheese. Whisk the egg white until stiff, then fold into the potato mixture. Spoon the potato mixture on top of the casserole and sprinkle with the remaining cheese.

6. Cook on 220°C + LOW for 10–15 minutes until golden brown.

BEEF ENCHILADAS

The strength of chilli sauces varies greatly. Use the amount we suggest, then taste the completed sauce. If it's not spicy enough, stir in extra chilli sauce.

Serves 4

1 large onion, finely chopped
2 garlic cloves, crushed
1 tsp oil
1 tbsp sweet chilli sauce
227 g can chopped tomatoes
Freshly milled salt and pepper
350 g/12 oz cooked beef, cut into thin strips
8 Mexican-style flour tortillas
115 g/4 oz grated Cheddar cheese

1. Put the onion, garlic and oil into a casserole. Cover and cook on HIGH for about 4 minutes until very soft. Stir in the chilli sauce and tomatoes. Cover and cook on HIGH for 3–5 minutes, stirring once. Season to taste.

2. Add half the sauce to the beef strips and stir to combine.

3. Put the tortillas on a plate. Cover with a damp paper towel, then with clear film. Cook on HIGH for 1 minute.

4. Spoon some of the beef sauce onto the top tortilla and quickly roll up like a Swiss-roll. Place in a flameproof dish. Repeat with the remaining tortillas and beef sauce. Spoon the tomato sauce over the rolls and sprinkle with the cheese.

MICROWAVE + GRILL:

5. Preheat the grill.

6. Stand the dish on a high rack. Put under the hot grill and cook on MED-LOW + GRILL for about 8–10 minutes or until golden brown.

COMBINATION:

5. Preheat the oven to 200°C.

6. Put into the hot oven and cook on 200°C + MED-LOW for about 8–10 minutes or until golden brown.

SPICY CURRIED MINCED BEEF

Based on a South African dish, boboutie. Serve with plenty of dressed green salad, buttered new potatoes or stir-fried cabbage.

Serves 4

55 g/2 oz brown bread
150 ml/¼ pint milk
1 large onion, finely chopped
1 tsp oil
350 g/12 oz extra-lean minced beef
2 tsp curry paste
½ tsp ground cinnamon
½ tsp ground turmeric
1 tbsp apricot jam
25 g/1 oz seedless raisins
2 tsp lemon juice
2 medium eggs, lightly beaten
2 tsp Dijon mustard
Freshly milled salt and pepper

1. Soak the bread in the milk for 5 minutes.

2. Put the onion and oil in an ovenproof casserole, cover and cook on HIGH for 3 minutes. Crumble in the beef and stir in the curry paste, spices, jam, raisins and lemon juice.

3. Squeeze out the bread, reserving the milk, and crumble it into the meat mixture. Cover and cook on HIGH for 9–10 minutes, stirring once or twice. Stir again and then level the surface.

4. Preheat the oven to 200°C.

5. Mix the reserved milk with the eggs, mustard and seasoning. Pour over the meat.

6. Put into the hot oven and cook on 200°C + MED-LOW for about 10 minutes or until the surface is just set. Cut into wedges for serving.

LAMB AND LEMON CASSEROLE

c

Delicious served with rice or new potatoes.

Serves 4

1 tbsp flour
6 tbsp finely chopped fresh mint
4 lean lamb chops
1 tbsp oil
1 medium onion, finely sliced
115 g/4 oz carrots, finely sliced
2 garlic cloves, crushed
227 g can chopped tomatoes
3 tbsp tomato purée
2 tsp sugar
75 ml/2½ fl oz dry white vermouth
Finely grated rind and juice of 1 large lemon

1. Put the flour and 2 tbsp of the mint into a large freezer bag and add the chops. Seal the opening and shake to coat the lamb chops evenly with the flour and herb. Heat half the oil in a non-stick frying pan (on the hob) and quickly brown the lamb on both sides.

2. Meanwhile, put the remaining oil, onion, carrots and garlic into a shallow casserole, large enough to hold the chops in a single layer. Cover and cook on HIGH for 4 minutes, stirring once, until soft. Combine the tomatoes, tomato purée, sugar, vermouth and lemon juice. Add to the casserole.

3. Cook on HIGH for about 2–3 minutes until the mixture just comes to the boil. Add the lamb chops, pushing them under the sauce.

4. Cover and cook on 180°C + MED-LOW for about 27–30 minutes until the lamb is tender.

5. Meanwhile, combine the lemon rind and remaining mint. Sprinkle on top of the casserole just before serving.

LAMB HOTPOT

A complete one-pot meal. Add a green vegetable or salad if wished.

To serve 2		To serve 4
15 g/½ oz	**butter**	*25 g/1 oz*
1 small	**onion, thinly sliced**	*1 medium*
115 g/4 oz	**carrots, diced**	*225 g/8 oz*
2	**celery sticks, thinly sliced**	*4*
225 g/8 oz	**lean lamb, cubed**	*450 g/1 lb*
4 tbsp	**dry white wine**	*85 ml/3 fl oz*
125 ml/4 fl oz	**lamb or vegetable stock**	*225 ml/8 fl oz*
1½ tbsp	**finely chopped fresh mint**	*3 tbsp*
	freshly milled salt and pepper	
225 g/8 oz	**baking potatoes, peeled and thinly sliced**	*450 g/1 lb*

1. Put half the butter into a casserole with the onion, carrots and celery. Cover and cook on HIGH for 2 minutes (*3 minutes*).

2. Add the lamb, wine, stock and mint. Season with salt and pepper.

3. Cover and cook on 180°C + HIGH for 5 minutes (*8 minutes*).

4. Put the remaining butter into a bowl and stand in the hot oven to melt. Stir the lamb mixture, then arrange the potato slices evenly on top. Drizzle over the melted butter.

5. Cover and cook on 180°C + MED-LOW for 15 minutes (*20 minutes*).

6. Remove the cover and continue to cook on 180°C + MED-LOW for about 10 minutes (*15 minutes*) or until the lamb is tender and the potatoes are soft and golden brown.

LAMB PAPRIKA WITH PARSLEY DUMPLINGS

Delicious and very satisfying; lightly-cooked finely-shredded cabbage would complete the meal nicely.

Serves 4

1 large onion, thinly sliced
1 garlic clove, crushed
1 tsp oil
1 medium red pepper, stalk and seeds removed and diced
Pinch of caraway seeds
2 tbsp mild paprika
675 g/1½ lb lean boneless lamb, cut into bite-size pieces
227 g can chopped tomatoes
300 ml/½ pint hot lamb or chicken stock
1 tbsp red wine vinegar
Freshly milled salt and pepper
115 g/4 oz self-raising flour
55 g/2 oz shredded vegetable suet
1 tbsp finely chopped fresh parsley

1. Put the onion, garlic and oil into a casserole. Cover and cook on HIGH for 3 minutes. Add the pepper, cover and cook for 2 minutes.

2. Stir in the caraway seeds, paprika and lamb. Add the tomatoes, stock and vinegar. Stir well. Cover and cook on 160°C + HIGH for about 5 minutes or until the stock just comes to the boil. Season and stir well.

3. Cover and cook on 160°C + MED-LOW for 18–20 minutes, stirring once, or until the lamb is tender.

4. Just before the lamb has finished cooking, sieve the flour and a pinch of salt into a bowl. Add the suet and parsley. Using a fork, stir in sufficient cold water to make a fairly stiff dough. With well-floured hands, shape into 8 balls.

5. Arrange on top of the meat, cover and cook on 160°C + MEDIUM for about 10 minutes or until the lamb is tender.

PORK CHOPS WITH PEACHES

Serve with rice (cooked before the casserole) or with mashed potato (cooked after the casserole) and a green vegetable.

To serve 2		To serve 4
1 medium	**onion, thinly sliced**	*1 large*
1 tsp	**oil**	*2 tsp*
1 tsp	**sugar**	*2 tsp*
2	**boneless pork chops**	*4*
240 g can	**peach halves in fruit juice**	*410 g can*
1 tbsp	**lemon juice**	*2 tbsp*
1 tbsp	**wholegrain mustard**	*2 tbsp*
	freshly milled salt and pepper	

1. Put the onion, oil and sugar into a shallow casserole. Cover and cook on HIGH for 2½ minutes *(4½ minutes)*, stirring once.

2. Meanwhile, quickly brown the chops on both sides in a non-stick frying pan (on the hob).

3. Drain the peach halves. Add the lemon juice, mustard and seasoning to 50 ml/2 fl oz *(100 ml/3½ fl oz)* of the juice.

4. Put the chops on top of the onions, tucking a peach half in between each chop. Pour over the seasoned juice. (Put any remaining fruit and juice into a non-metal container and refrigerate for another recipe.)

5. Cover and cook on 200°C + MED-LOW for about 14–15 minutes *(18–20 minutes)* or until the pork is tender.

PORK AND POTATO PAPRIKA [C]

Just add a lightly cooked green vegetable such as broccoli or finely shredded Savoy cabbage. This recipe could also be made with cubed baking potatoes, in place of new potatoes.

To serve 2		To serve 4
2	**boneless pork chops**	4
1 tsp	**oil**	2 tsp
1 medium	**onion, thinly sliced**	1 large
1 tsp	**sugar**	2 tsp
2 tsp	**plain flour**	1 tbsp
1 tbsp	**tomato purée**	2 tbsp
2 tsp	**paprika**	1 tbsp
2 tsp	**red wine vinegar**	1 tbsp
150 ml/¼ pint	**hot vegetable stock**	300 ml/½ pint
	freshly milled salt and pepper	
225 g/8 oz	**small new potatoes, quartered**	450 g/1 lb
85 ml/3 fl oz	**natural yogurt**	150 ml/¼ pint
1 tbsp	**mango chutney**	2 tbsp

1. Quickly brown the chops on both sides in a non-stick frying pan (on the hob) over a high heat.

2. Meanwhile, put the oil, onion, and sugar into a shallow casserole. Cover and cook on HIGH for 3 minutes *(5 minutes)*, stirring once, or until soft. Stir in the flour, tomato purée, paprika and vinegar. Gradually stir in the hot stock.

3. Cook on HIGH for 2 minutes *(3 minutes)* or until the mixture comes to the boil. Season and stir well. Add the potatoes, stirring to coat them with the sauce. Add the chops, spooning potatoes and sauce over the top of them.

4. Cover and cook on 200°C + MED-LOW for about 15 minutes *(20 minutes)* or until the pork and potatoes are tender.

5. Combine the yogurt and mango chutney (finely chopping any large pieces of mango) and serve with the pork.

PORK, APPLE AND PARSNIP CASSEROLE

A delicious meal-in-one-dish, just add a lightly cooked vegetable such as cabbage or Brussels sprouts.

Serves 4

900 g/2 lb parsnips, sliced
2 medium onions, thinly sliced
1 tsp oil
550 g/1¼ lb minced pork
1 Bramley apple, peeled, cored and sliced
150 ml/¼ pint apple juice
1 vegetable stock cube
1 tbsp wholegrain mustard
Freshly milled salt and pepper
55 g/2 oz grated Cheshire cheese

1. Put the parsnips and 5 tbsp water into a casserole. Cover and cook on HIGH for 10–15 minutes, stirring once, or until just tender. Leave to stand.

2. Put the onions and oil into a casserole. Cover and cook on HIGH for 3–4 minutes. Break up the mince with a fork and add to the casserole with the apple.

3. Cover and cook on HIGH for 5 minutes, stirring once. Add the apple juice, crumbled stock cube and mustard. Stir well.

4. Cover and cook on HIGH for 2–3 minutes. Stir.

5. Cover and cook on MED-HIGH for about 12 minutes. Season to taste. Spoon into a shallow flameproof dish.

6. Meanwhile, drain and mash the parsnips. Season to taste. Spoon on top of the pork and sprinkle the cheese on top.

MICROWAVE + GRILL:

7. Stand on a high rack and cook on MEDIUM + GRILL for about 7–8 minutes or until golden brown.

COMBINATION:

7. Preheat the oven to 200°C.

8. Put into the hot oven and cook on 200°C + MED-LOW for about 10 minutes or until golden brown.

LEEK AND BACON PIE

Ready-to-roll shortcrust pastry is available chilled or frozen. Thaw frozen pastry, following packet instructions, before use. Serve with a lightly-cooked green vegetable.

Serves 4

115 g/4 oz lean back bacon, chopped
1 tbsp butter
225 g/8 oz leeks, thinly sliced
25 g/1 oz plain flour
300 ml/½ pint milk
Freshly milled salt and pepper
250g shortcrust pastry
4 medium eggs
Beaten egg, to brush

1. Put the bacon and butter into a casserole, cover and cook on HIGH for 1½–2 minutes. Add the leeks, cover and cook on HIGH for 3 minutes, stirring once. Stir in the flour and gradually blend in the milk. Cook on HIGH for about 4–5 minutes, stirring frequently, until the sauce just comes to the boil and is thickened and smooth. Season to taste. Tip into a 23 cm/9 inch ovenproof flan dish and leave to cool.

2. Preheat the oven to 220°C. Roll out the pastry slightly larger than 23 cm/9 inches.

3. Crack one egg into a small dish. Make a well in the sauce and slide the egg into it. Repeat with the remaining eggs. Prick the yolks with a skewer or cocktail stick.

4. Brush the edges of the dish with cold water and top with the pastry. Fold the edges under and pinch together to seal them well. Slash the top of the pie and brush the pastry with beaten egg.

5. Put into the hot oven and cook on 220°C + MED-LOW for about 18–20 minutes until crisp and golden brown.

BACON AND VEGETABLE PIE

Serves 4

1 large onion, thinly sliced
1 tsp oil
2 medium parsnips, diced
3 medium carrots, sliced
55 g/2 oz sweetcorn
400 g/14 oz cooked bacon or ham, cubed
300 g can condensed cream of mushroom soup
50 ml/2 fl oz milk
225 g/8 oz puff pastry, thawed if frozen
Beaten egg, to brush

1. Put the onion and oil into a casserole. Cover and cook on HIGH for 3 minutes. Stir in the parsnips and carrots, cover and cook for 5 minutes, stirring once. Add the sweetcorn and bacon. Stir until combined, then spoon into a 23 cm/9 inch ovenproof flan dish.

2. Preheat the oven to 220°C.

3. Combine the soup and milk and pour over the vegetables and bacon.

4. Roll out the pastry and cut to fit the top of the dish, plus a strip to fit around the edge of the dish. Dampen the edge of the dish and fit the pastry strip in place. Dampen the pastry strip, top with the circle of pastry and pinch the edges together. Decorate the top of the pie with pastry trimmings, if wished, and cut a small slit in the top to allow the steam to escape. Brush the pastry with beaten egg.

5. Put into the hot oven and cook on 220°C + MED-LOW for about 18–20 minutes or until the pastry is puffed and golden brown.

SAUSAGE AND DUMPLING HOTPOT

A simple, satisfying dish – good served with broccoli.

Serves 4

450 g/1 lb pork sausages
225 g/8 oz lean gammon steak, cut into bit-sized pieces
1 tsp oil
2 large onions, thinly sliced
2 tbsp plain flour
600 ml/1 pint vegetable stock
Freshly milled salt and pepper
4 tbsp chopped fresh parsley
115 g/4 oz self-raising flour
55 g/2 oz shredded vegetable suet

1. Cook the sausages in a non-stick frying pan (on the hob) until golden brown. Drain on paper towels.

2. Put the gammon, oil and onions into a casserole. Cover and cook on HIGH for about 5 minutes, stirring once, until the onions are very soft. Stir in the plain flour, then the stock. Cook on HIGH for about 3–4 minutes, stirring once, until the sauce just comes to the boil and is thickened. Season and stir in half the parsley. Add the sausages to the casserole, pushing them under the surface of the sauce.

3. Cover and cook on 200°C + MEDIUM for 10 minutes.

4. Meanwhile, put the self-raising flour and a pinch of salt in a bowl. Season with pepper, add the remaining parsley and the suet. Stir in sufficient cold water to form a soft dough. Shape into 8 balls.

5. Arrange the dumplings on top of the sausages, cover and cook on 200°C + MEDIUM for 8–10 minutes until risen and piping hot.

7

POULTRY

As in the meat chapter we've used all the functions of the combination cooker to give tasty, versatile dishes. Dip Chicken Fingers into Minted Yogurt Dip, or a portion of Turkey Moussaka, or, for something special, try Caramelised Duck with Orange Sauce.

In some recipes which use microwave + grill, we recommend using a high rack for two-portion dishes and a low rack for four, to ensure that food in the larger dishes is fully cooked or heated without the top becoming too brown. The first time you make a dish, keep an eye on it – some grills brown quicker than others.

TURKEY MOUSSAKA

Some crisp rolls and a garlicky salad would complement this well-flavoured dish.

To serve 2		To serve 4
1	aubergine(s), about 350 g/12 oz each	2
	oil (or spray can)	
115 g/4 oz	minced turkey	225 g/8 oz
300 ml/½ pint	milk	600 ml/1 pint
25 g/1 oz	plain flour	55 g/2 oz
25 g/1 oz	butter	55 g/2 oz
85 g/3 oz	Mozzarella cheese, thinly sliced	140 g/5 oz
1 tbsp	finely chopped fresh (or frozen) basil	2 tbsp
	freshly milled salt and pepper	
2 large	tomatoes, peeled and thinly sliced	4 large
half a 50 g can	anchovies, drained	50 g can
2 tbsp	grated Parmesan cheese	4 tbsp

1. Cut the aubergine(s) into thin slices, discarding the stem. Arrange in a single layer on a grill pan and lightly brush with oil (or use a spray can). Grill until the aubergine is browned, turning once (you may need to do this in batches). Cook the minced turkey in a non-stick frying pan with a little oil until browned.

2. Put the milk and flour into a bowl and whisk until smooth. Add the butter. Cook on HIGH for about 2 minutes (3 minutes), whisking frequently, until the sauce comes to the boil and is thickened and smooth. Add the Mozzarella cheese and stir until melted. Add the basil and season to taste.

3. Layer the aubergines, tomatoes and turkey in a lightly buttered shallow flameproof dish, then pour over the sauce. Top with the anchovies and Parmesan cheese.

MICROWAVE + GRILL:

4. Stand the dish on a high *(low)* rack. Cook on MEDIUM + GRILL for about 10 minutes *(15 minutes)* or until bubbling hot and golden brown.

COMBINATION:

4. Preheat the oven to 200°C.

5. Put into the hot oven and cook on 200°C + MEDIUM for about 10 minutes *(15 minutes)* or until bubbling hot and golden brown.

CHICKEN AND ARTICHOKES AU GRATIN

Good served with lightly cooked green beans, courgettes or peas.

To serve 2		To serve 4
2	**skinned and boned chicken breasts**	4
100 ml/3½ fl oz	**chicken stock**	200 ml/7 fl oz
25 g/1 oz	**butter**	55 g/2 oz
1 large	**fresh bread slice(s), diced**	2 large
1 tbsp	**finely chopped fresh parsley**	2 tbsp
150 ml/¼ pint	**milk**	300 ml/½ pint
1½ tbsp	**plain flour**	3 tbsp
Pinch	**grated nutmeg**	¼ tsp
55 g/2 oz	**grated smoked Cheddar cheese**	85 g/3 oz
	salt and freshly milled pepper	
4 (canned)	**artichoke hearts, halved**	400 g can

1. Put the chicken into a shallow flameproof dish and pour over the stock. Cover and cook on MED-HIGH for about 6 minutes *(8 minutes)* or until just cooked through. Lift the chicken onto a plate, reserving the stock.

2. Put the butter into a bowl. Cook on HIGH for 20 seconds *(1 minute)* until melted. Add half to the bread cubes and mix with a fork until the cubes are evenly coated with the butter. Stir in the parsley.

3. Add the milk and reserved stock to the remaining butter. Whisk in the flour and nutmeg until smooth. Cook on HIGH for 2 minutes *(3 minutes),* stirring frequently, or until the sauce comes to the boil and is thickened and smooth. Add the cheese and stir until melted. Season to taste.

4. Cut the chicken into bite-sized pieces and add to the sauce with the artichokes Stir gently to combine, then spoon into the flame-proof dish (the one in which the chicken was cooked).

5. Spoon the buttered bread cubes on top of the chicken.

MICROWAVE + GRILL:

6. Preheat the grill.

7. Stand the dish on a high *(low)* rack. Cook on MED-LOW + GRILL for about 5 minutes *(8 minutes)* or until the topping is golden brown.

COMBINATION:

6. Preheat the oven to 200°C.

7. Put into the hot oven and cook on 200°C + MED-LOW for about 10 minutes *(15 minutes)* or until the topping is golden brown.

CHICKEN, CHIVE AND MUSHROOM CASSEROLE

There is a lot of delicious creamy sauce in this casserole so serve it with jacket or mashed potatoes, rice or pasta. No chives? Use freeze-dried mixed herbs.

To serve 2		To serve 4
1 small	**onion, thinly sliced**	*1 medium*
1	**garlic clove(s), crushed**	*2*
1 tsp	**oil**	*1 tsp*
2	**skinned and boned chicken breasts, cut into bite-size pieces**	*4*
1½ tbsp	**flour**	*3 tbsp*
1 tbsp	**finely chopped chives**	*2 tbsp*
85 ml/3 fl oz	**hot chicken stock**	*150 ml/¼ pint*
85 ml/3 fl oz	**dry white vermouth**	*150 ml/¼ pint*
2 tsp	**lemon juice**	*1 tbsp*
	freshly milled salt and pepper	
115 g/4 oz	**baby button mushrooms**	*225 g/8 oz*
85 ml/3 fl oz	**soured or double cream**	*150 ml/¼ pint*

1. Put the onion, garlic and oil into an ovenproof casserole. Cover and cook on HIGH for 2 minutes *(3 minutes)* until soft.

2. Add the chicken pieces, cover and cook on HIGH for 2 minutes *(3 minutes)*. Stir in the flour, then the herbs, stock, vermouth, lemon juice, seasoning and mushrooms.

3. Cover and cook on 160°C + HIGH for 5 minutes *(8 minutes)*. Stir well, cover and cook on 160°C + MEDIUM for about 10 minutes *(15 minutes)*, stirring once, until the chicken is cooked.

4. Stir in the cream, cover and continue to cook on 160°C + MEDIUM for about 4–5 minutes *(7–8 minutes)*. Stir, check the seasoning and serve.

CARAMELISED DUCK WITH ORANGE SAUCE

A very special duck dish – add egg thread noodles, tossed with a little soy sauce, plus some lightly-cooked mangetout.

To serve 2		To serve 4
2	**duck breasts, about 175 g/6 oz each**	*4*
2 tsp	**sugar**	*4 tsp*
75 ml/2½ fl oz	**orange juice**	*125 ml/4 fl oz*
75 ml/2½ fl oz	**dry white vermouth**	*125 ml/4 fl oz*
2 tbsp	**orange marmalade**	*3 tbsp*
1 tsp	**cornflour**	*2 tsp*
	freshly milled salt and pepper	

1. Preheat the grill.

2. With a very sharp knife, score the duck skin into diamonds. Put the duck in a single layer in a shallow flameproof dish. Rub the sugar into the skin. Stand the dish on a high rack and put under the hot grill for about 7–8 minutes *(9–10 minutes)*. Pour off and reserve the juices.

3. Mix together the juice, vermouth, marmalade and reserved juices. Pour around the duck (make sure the duck is skin-side up).

4. Stand the dish on a high *(low)* rack and cook on MED-LOW + GRILL for about 6 minutes *(9 minutes)* or until the duck is crisp and just cooked.

5. Lift the duck out and keep hot. Spoon off and discard the fat from the top of the sauce. Mix the cornflour with a little cold water to make a smooth paste and stir into the sauce. Cook on HIGH for about 1 minute *(1½ minutes)* or until thickened and bubbling. Season to taste and serve with the duck.

SPICED CHICKEN ON RATATOUILLE

Lots of delicious sauce – serve with mashed potatoes or hot rice.

To serve 2		To serve 4
2	**chicken leg quarters**	*4*
1 tsp	**dried mixed herbs**	*1 tbsp*
1 tsp	**ground coriander**	*1 tbsp*
½ tsp	**paprika**	*1 tsp*
	freshly milled salt and pepper	
½	**finely grated rind and juice of lemon**	*1*
400 g can	**ratatouille**	*two 400 g cans*

1. Trim off and discard any excess fat and skin from the chicken. Put the herbs, spices and seasoning into a food (freezer) bag and add the chicken. Shake well until the chicken is evenly coated.

2. Stir the lemon rind and juice into the ratatouille and spread the mixture in a shallow flameproof dish, just large enough to hold the chicken. Arrange the chicken, skinned side up, on top.

3. Put onto a low rack and cook on MEDIUM + GRILL *(MED-HIGH + GRILL)* for 15–20 minutes or until the chicken is crisp, golden and cooked through. (If the chicken looks like browning too quickly, move the dish from the rack and onto the oven base/turntable.)

CHICKEN KORMA

A mild creamy curry. Serve with poppadums and a spicy mango chutney.

To serve 2		*To serve 4*
55 g/2 oz	**ground almonds**	*115 g/4 oz*
1 tbsp	**mild or medium curry paste**	*2 tbsp*
1 tsp	**oil**	*2 tsp*
1 medium	**onion, thinly sliced**	*1 large*
350 g/12 oz	**skinless boneless chicken (breast and/or thighs), cut into bite-size pieces**	*675 g/1½ lb*
3 tbsp	**natural yogurt**	*6 tbsp*
	freshly milled salt and pepper	
3 tbsp	**double cream**	*6 tbsp*
1 tbsp	**chopped fresh coriander**	*2 tbsp*
	lemon wedges, to serve	

1. Combine the almonds and curry paste and stir in 75 ml/2½ fl oz *(150 ml/¼ pint)* water.

2. Put the oil and onion into an ovenproof casserole, cover and cook on HIGH for 2 minutes *(3 minutes)*.

3. Stir in the chicken, almond mixture, yogurt and seasoning. Cover and cook on 200°C + HIGH for about 4 minutes *(5–6 minutes)* or until the mixture just comes to the boil.

4. Stir, cover and cook on 200°C + MED-LOW for about 15 minutes *(18–20 minutes)*, stirring once or twice, or until the chicken is tender.

5. Stir in the cream and coriander. Serve with the lemon wedges.

STUFFED TURKEY ROLLS
IN HERB AND TOMATO SAUCE

Serve with mashed potatoes and a lightly-cooked green vegetable such as buttered courgettes.

Serves 4

1 tsp oil
1 small onion, finely chopped
1 tsp fennel seeds
1 tbsp tomato purée
3 sausages, skinned
Freshly milled salt and pepper
4 turkey fillets
2 garlic cloves, crushed
1 tbsp finely chopped fresh sage
1 tsp finely chopped fresh rosemary
150 ml/¼ pint dry white wine or vermouth
227 g can chopped tomatoes
8 pitted black olives

1. Put the oil and onion into a small casserole. Cover and cook on HIGH for 2 minutes. Stir in the fennel seeds and tomato purée and leave to cool slightly. Break up the sausages with a fork and stir into the onion mixture. Season with salt and pepper.

2. Using a rolling pin, flatten the turkey fillets between sheets of non-stick paper. Cover each fillet evenly with the sausage mixture, roll up and secure with wooden cocktail sticks.

3. Put the garlic, herbs, wine and tomatoes into a casserole, large enough to hold the turkey rolls in a single layer. Add the turkey, spooning the sauce over the top of them.

4. Cover and cook on 200°C + MED-LOW for about 20–25 minutes, turning the rolls over halfway, until the turkey is tender.

5. Remove the cocktail sticks and slice each turkey roll diagonally. Add the olives to the sauce and spoon around the turkey.

CHICKEN FINGERS WITH MINTED YOGURT DIP

Moist fingers of tender chicken, marinated then given a crisp coating of herb breadcrumbs and cooked very quickly in the combination cooker. Prepare everything ahead and then cook the chicken at the last minute so that it is served piping hot. Pile the chicken in a basket with potato crisps and add a simple salad of cherry tomatoes and celery sticks.

Serves 2

150 ml/¼ pint natural yogurt
1 garlic clove, crushed
Finely grated rind and juice of ½ lemon
1 tbsp tomato purée
Freshly milled salt and pepper
2 skinned and boned chicken breasts
1 tbsp mint jelly
55 g/2 oz fresh breadcrumbs
1 tbsp dried mixed herbs

1. Put half the yogurt into a medium bowl and add the garlic, lemon rind and juice, tomato purée, salt and pepper. Whisk until smooth.

2. Cut each chicken breast into six fingers and place in a food (freezer) bag. Add the yogurt mixture. Seal the bag and shake to coat the chicken evenly with the marinade. Refrigerate for 2–3 hours or overnight, turning once or twice.

3. Into the remaining yogurt, whisk the mint jelly and seasoning to taste. Cover and chill until needed.

4. On a sheet of greaseproof paper combine the breadcrumbs and herbs. Using a fork, lift each piece of chicken onto the crumbs and turn to coat on all sides. Arrange on a flat flameproof plate.

5. Preheat the grill.

6. Stand the plate on a high rack. Put under the hot grill and cook on MED-LOW + GRILL for about 10 minutes, turning the pieces over half way, or until the chicken is cooked through. Serve with the yogurt dip.

CHICKEN-STUFFED AUBERGINE

Add some crusty garlic bread and a green salad for a very satisfying meal.

To serve 2		To serve 4
1	**aubergine(s), about 450 g/1 lb each**	*2*
1 tsp	**oil**	*2 tsp*
1 small	**onion, finely chopped**	*1 medium*
1 tbsp	**tomato purée**	*2 tbsp*
2 tbsp	**finely chopped fresh parsley**	*4 tbsp*
55 g/2 oz	**fresh breadcrumbs**	*115 g/4 oz*
	freshly milled salt and pepper	
175 g/6 oz	**cooked chicken fillet, finely chopped**	*350 g/12 oz*
55 g/2 oz	**Cheddar cheese, thinly sliced**	*115 g/4 oz*

1. Halve the aubergine(s) lengthways, discarding the stem(s). Scoop out the flesh leaving a 1 cm/½ inch thick shell. Finely chop the flesh.

2. Put the oil and onion into a casserole. Cover and cook on HIGH for 1 minute *(2 minutes)*. Stir in the chopped aubergine, tomato purée, parsley and breadcrumbs. Cover and cook on HIGH for 2 minutes *(3 minutes)*. Season to taste. Stir in the chopped chicken.

3. Put the aubergine shells into a shallow flameproof dish and fill them with the stuffing. Top with the cheese and spoon 3 tbsp *(6 tbsp)* water into the dish around the aubergine(s).

MICROWAVE + GRILL:

4. Stand the dish on a high *(low)* rack. Cook on MED-LOW + GRILL for about 15 minutes *(20–25 minutes)* or until the aubergine is soft when pierced with a fork and the tops are golden brown.

COMBINATION:

4. Cook on 200°C + MEDIUM for about 15 minutes *(25 minutes)* or until the aubergine is soft when pierced with a fork and the tops are golden brown.

TURKEY AND VEGETABLE GRATIN

Chunks of turkey and vegetables in a creamy herb sauce topped with crunchy golden croûtons. Just add a crisp green salad tossed with your favourite dressing.

To serve 2		To serve 4
25 g/1 oz	**butter**	*55 g/2 oz*
2 large	**fresh bread slices, diced**	*4 large*
1 small	**onion, thinly sliced**	*1 medium*
2 small	**carrots, thinly sliced**	*3 medium*
2	**celery sticks, thinly sliced**	*4*
280 g/10 oz	**turkey breast fillet, cut into bite-size pieces**	*550 g/1¼ lb*
150 ml/¼ pint	**chicken stock**	*300 ml/½ pint*
50 g/1½ oz	**soft cheese with garlic and herbs**	*100 g/3½ oz*
	freshly milled salt and pepper	
	paprika	

1. Put the butter in a flameproof casserole and cook on HIGH for 20 seconds *(30 seconds)* or until melted. Add all but 1 tsp *(1 tbsp)* to the bread cubes and toss with a fork until evenly mixed.

2. To the butter remaining in the casserole, add the onion, carrots and celery. Cover and cook for 3 minutes *(4 minutes)*, stirring once. Add the turkey and stock.

3. Cover and cook on HIGH for about 3 minutes *(5 minutes)* until just bubbling around the edges. Stir well, then continue cooking on MEDIUM for about 8 minutes *(10–12 minutes)*, stirring once, until the turkey is just tender.

4. Stir in the cheese and adjust the seasoning. Spoon the buttered bread cubes evenly on top of the turkey and vegetables. Sprinkle with paprika.

5. Stand the dish on a low rack. Cook on MED-LOW + GRILL for about 6 minutes *(8 minutes)* until golden brown.

CHICKEN EN CROÛTE WITH PARSLEY AND LEMON

Tender chicken in a crisp pastry case – good with new potatoes, tossed with melted butter, and peas.

Serves 2

4 tbsp finely chopped fresh parsley
2 tbsp grated Parmesan cheese
2 tbsp ground almonds
1 garlic clove, crushed
Finely grated rind and juice of 1 lemon
Freshly milled salt and pepper
225 g/8 oz puff pastry, thawed if frozen
2 skinned and boned chicken breasts
1 medium egg, beaten

1. Put the parsley, cheese, almonds, garlic and lemon rind into a bowl. Mix well. Work in enough lemon juice to make a soft paste. Season with salt and pepper.

2. Roll out the pastry, trim the edges and cut into two 20 cm/8 inch squares.

3. Place half the parsley mixture in the centre of one piece of pastry and place a chicken breast on top of each. Brush the edges of the pastry with egg and fold up like a parcel, pressing the seams to seal them. Repeat with the remaining parsley mixture, chicken and pastry.

4. Place the pastry parcels on a flat ovenproof dish. Brush with egg, decorate with pastry trimmings and make several small cuts in the top of the pastry. Chill for at least 1 hour.

5. Preheat the oven to 200°C.

6. Put into the hot oven and cook on 200°C + MED-LOW for about 15–18 minutes until golden brown and cooked through.

8

CAKES, BAKES AND PASTRIES

Cakes and pastry are very successful in the combination cooker – the microwaves ensure a good rise and light texture, while the heat crisps and browns the outer layers to give that traditional golden-brown crust.

Before using a recipe, read page 12, regarding the kind of cooking containers to use.

Recipes for Easy Crisp Pastry and Sweet Crisp pastry are so easy to prepare and use. There's no rolling out, just press the mixture into an ovenproof flan dish. If a pre-baked pastry case is required and you are using a store-bought version, carefully remove it from the foil container and slide it into a suitably-sized flan or pie dish, or stand it on a flat plate before adding the filling. Chilled or frozen pastry is also worth trying.

If the manufacturer of your cooker recommends the use of metal baking dishes when cooking on combination, do remember that our cooking times have been developed using ovenproof glass containers. The latter allow microwaves to enter the food from all angles to give a successful rise and an even texture – with a shorter cooking time. With metal dishes, you may need to increase the cooking time, and the final texture and appearance may be affected.

In this chapter, you will not find really rich fruit cakes – they need to be cooked slowly on convection-only to achieve that rich, dark and moist texture that we have come to expect of them. Similarly, small items such as individual cakes and scones are best cooked on convection.

Many of the recipes in this chapter are cooked in a preheated (hot) oven – so remember to set your cooker appropriately.

MIXED FRUIT CAKE

C

Makes 8–10 slices

225 g/8 oz self-raising flour
115 g/4 oz caster sugar
175 g/6 oz soft tub margarine
2 medium eggs, beaten
50 ml/2 fl oz milk
55 g/2 oz dried ready-to-eat apricots, chopped
55 g/2 oz stoned dates, chopped
55 g/2 oz sultanas
Clear honey
Demerara sugar

1. Lightly grease an 18 cm/7 inch ovenproof soufflé dish and line the base with non-stick paper.

2. Sift the flour into a bowl and add the sugar, margarine, eggs and milk. With an electric mixer or wooden spoon, beat until light and fluffy. Stir in the fruit. Spoon the mixture into the dish and level the top.

3. Cook on 180°C + LOW for about 40–45 minutes or until a skewer, inserted in the centre of the cake, comes out clean.

4. Leave to cool for 15 minutes, then turn the cake out onto a wire rack. Lightly brush the top with honey and sprinkle with demerara sugar. Cool completely before cutting into wedges.

WALNUT AND CARROT CAKE WITH CREAM CHEESE FROSTING

Do take the time to grate the carrot finely as this makes such a difference to the texture of the cake.

Makes 8–10 slices

175 g/6 oz soft butter
175 g/6 oz soft brown sugar
3 medium eggs, beaten
175 g/6 oz finely grated carrots
Finely grated rind of 1 lemon
175 g/6 oz self-raising flour
½ tsp baking powder
50 g/1¾ oz broken walnuts
115 g/4 oz cream cheese
2 tbsp lemon curd
225 g/8 oz sifted icing sugar
8–10 walnut halves

1. Lightly grease a deep 20 cm/8 inch ovenproof flan dish and line the base with non-stick paper. Preheat the oven to 180°C.

2. Beat the butter and sugar together until light and fluffy. Gradually beat in the eggs, carrots and lemon rind.

3. Sift over the flour and baking powder. Beat until smooth. Stir in the walnuts. Spoon into the dish and level the top.

4. Put into the hot oven and cook on 180°C + MED-LOW for about 18–20 minutes or until cooked (a skewer inserted in the centre should come out clean). Leave to cool for 5 minutes before turning out onto a wire rack and removing the paper. Cool completely.

5. Put the cream cheese into a bowl and warm on MEDIUM for about 1 minute until soft. Beat in the lemon curd, then the sifted icing sugar, whisking until smooth and creamy. Swirl the mixture on top of the cold cake and decorate with the walnut halves.

CRUNCHY DATE SLICES

A family favourite – but baked in less than 20 minutes. Good served cold, or warm as dessert with a scoop of ice cream or with custard.

Makes 8–10 slices

250 g/9 oz dried ready-to-eat dates
Finely grated rind and juice of 1 large lemon
150 g/5½ oz soft butter
70 g/2½ oz caster sugar
200 g/7 oz plain flour
35 g/1¼ oz semolina

1. Finely chop the dates, removing any stones. Put the dates, lemon rind, lemon juice and 4 tbsp water into a casserole. Cover and cook on MED-HIGH for 2 minutes. Stir until smooth. Leave until lukewarm.

2. Preheat the oven to 220°C.

3. Beat together the butter and sugar until light and fluffy. Sift over the flour, add the semolina and stir in to form coarse crumbs.

4. Press half the dough into a 20 cm/8 inch ovenproof flan dish and spoon the date mixture on top. Spoon the remaining dough evenly on top of the dates and press down lightly.

5. Put into the hot oven and cook on 220°C + MED-LOW for about 15 minutes or until lightly browned and just firm.

6. To serve warm, leave to cool for 10 minutes before cutting into wedges. To serve cold, leave to cool for 10 minutes then cut into wedges. Leave to cool completely before removing from the dish.

STICKY TOFFEE CAKE

If you like the pudding – you will love the cake!

Makes 8 slices

250 g/9 oz stoned dates
1 tsp bicarbonate of soda
140 g/5 oz soft brown sugar
55 g/2 oz soft tub margarine
1 medium egg
200 g/7 oz plain flour
1 tsp baking powder
25 g/1 oz broken walnuts

Topping:
5 tbsp soft brown sugar
5 tbsp whipping cream
25 g/1 oz butter

1. Roughly chop the dates into a bowl and pour over 225 ml/8 fl oz boiling water. Add the soda and stir well. Cook on HIGH for 1 minute. Stir, then leave to cool.

2. Preheat the oven to 180°C. Lightly grease a 23 cm/9 inch ovenproof flan dish.

3. Put the sugar, margarine and egg into a bowl. With an electric mixer or wooden spoon, beat until smooth and creamy. Sift over the flour and baking powder. Beat until smooth. Add the date mixture and nuts and stir until well combined. Spoon into the dish and level the top.

4. Put into the hot oven and cook on 180°C + MED-LOW for about 15 minutes or until just firm to the touch. Stand on a wire rack.

5. Make the topping. Put the sugar, cream and butter into a bowl. Cook on HIGH for about 1 minute until bubbling. Stir well, then pour evenly over the hot cake.

6. Leave in the dish until completely cold before cutting into wedges.

SHORTBREAD

For speed, use a food processor. Buzz the butter, sugar and vanilla until creamy, add the dry ingredients and buzz briefly until combined. Do not over-process. Tip the mixture onto the work surface, gather into a ball, knead briefly until smooth and continue as below. When making the recipes containing chopped nuts, chop them in the processor first, tip them out before creaming the soft ingredients, then add with the dry ingredients.

Makes 8–10 wedges

150 g/5½ oz soft butter
70 g/2½ oz caster sugar
1 tsp vanilla extract
200 g/7 oz plain flour
35 g/1¼ oz semolina or ground rice

1. Preheat the oven to 200°C.

2. Beat together the butter, sugar and vanilla until fluffy. Sift over the flour, add the semolina or ground rice and stir in. Gather the dough into a smooth ball.

3. Press the dough into a 20 cm/8 inch ovenproof flan dish and level the surface. Using a fork or fingers, mark a pretty border around the edge. Prick the centre with a fork.

4. Put into the hot oven and cook on 200°C + MED-LOW for about 8–10 minutes or until lightly browned and just firm.

5. Leave to cool for 5 minutes then cut into wedges. Cool completely before removing from the dish.

NUTTY SHORTBREAD

150 g/5½ oz soft butter
70 g/2½ oz caster or soft brown sugar
1 tsp vanilla extract
150 g/5½ oz plain flour
50 g/1/¾ oz ground almonds or very finely chopped toasted
    hazelnuts or walnuts
35 g/1¼ oz semolina or ground rice

Follow the method on page 128, adding the nuts with the semolina
or ground rice.

ORANGE SHORTBREAD

Use the ingredients as for plain Shortbread and add the finely grated
rind of 1 orange to the butter, sugar and vanilla before beating until
light and fluffy.

CHOCOLATE AND ORANGE CAKE

If you like, drizzle orange glacé icing over the top of the cooled cake.

Serves 8–10

200 g/7 oz self-raising flour
2 tsp baking powder
175 g/6 oz soft tub margarine
175 g/6 oz soft brown sugar
3 medium eggs, beaten
Finely grated rind of 1 medium orange
3 tbsp orange juice
85 g/3 oz plain chocolate, grated

1. Lightly butter a 20 cm/8 inch ovenproof soufflé or cake dish and line the base with non-stick paper. Preheat the oven to 200°C.

2. Put all the ingredients into a large bowl and beat until well combined. Spoon into the dish and level the top.

3. Put into the hot oven and cook on 200°C + MED-LOW for about 18–20 minutes until well risen and just firm to the touch.

4. Leave to cool for 5 minutes, then turn out onto a wire rack to cool completely.

BAKEWELL TART

Equally good served warm with cream, or cold.

Makes 6 slices

2 tbsp raspberry jam
20 cm/8 inch pre-baked sweet pastry case
55 g/2 oz soft butter
55 g/2 oz caster sugar
1 medium egg, lightly beaten
Few drops of almond extract
25 g/1 oz self-raising flour
½ tsp baking powder
55 g/2 oz ground almonds
2 tsp milk
2 tbsp flaked almonds

1. Preheat the oven to 220°C.

2. Spread the jam carefully over the base of the pastry case.

3. Beat together the butter and sugar until light and fluffy. Gradually beat in the egg and almond extract. Sift over the flour and baking powder. Add the ground almonds and milk. Using a metal spoon, fold in until smooth. Spread the mixture over the jam in the pastry case, gently levelling the surface. Scatter the flaked almonds around the edge.

4. Put into the hot oven and cook on 220°C + MED-LOW for about 10 minutes or until set and golden brown.

5. Allow to cool slightly before cutting into wedges.

COFFEE WALNUT CAKE

The traditional combination of coffee and walnuts makes this cake perfect for a special tea.

Makes 8–10 slices

175 g/6 oz soft margarine
175 g/6 oz soft brown sugar
3 medium eggs
2 tbsp very strong black coffee
175 g/6 oz self-raising flour
½ tsp baking powder
25 g/1 oz chopped walnuts

Buttercream:
115 g/4 oz soft butter
225 g/8 oz sifted icing sugar
1 tbsp very strong black coffee

Icing:
175 g/6 oz sifted icing sugar
1–2 tbsp very strong black coffee
Walnut halves, to decorate

1. Preheat the oven to 200°C. Line the base of a deep 20 cm/8 inch ovenproof flan dish with non-stick paper.

2. Put the margarine and sugar into a bowl and, with an electric mixer or wooden spoon, beat until light and fluffy. Beat in the eggs and coffee. Sift over the flour and baking powder and beat thoroughly until the mixture is smooth and light. Stir in the walnuts.

3. Spoon into the dish and level the top. Put into the hot oven and cook on 200°C + MED-LOW for about 15 minutes or until well risen and firm when lightly pressed with a fingertip. Leave to stand for 5 minutes, then turn out onto a wire rack. Leave until cold.

4. *Buttercream:* Put the butter, icing sugar and coffee into a bowl and beat until very smooth. Carefully split the cold cake horizontally into two layers. Spread the buttercream on one cut side and replace the second layer. Stand the cake on a wire rack.

5. *Coffee icing:* Put the icing sugar into a bowl and gradually beat in teaspoonfuls of coffee to make smooth icing that will just spread. Pour the icing on top of the cake and quickly spread it so that it just drizzles down the sides of the cake. Arrange the walnut halves on top and leave to stand for 3–4 hours until the icing is quite set.

CHOCOLATE AND CARAMEL SHORTBREAD

Makes 8–10 wedges

200 g/7 oz soft butter
70 g/2½ oz caster sugar
1 tsp vanilla extract
200 g/7 oz plain flour
35 g/1¼ oz ground rice
55 g/2 oz soft brown sugar
397 g can condensed milk
100 g/3½ oz plain chocolate

1. Preheat the oven to 200°C. Line the base of a 20 cm/8 inch ovenproof flan dish with non-stick paper.

2. Put 150 g/5½ oz of the butter, the caster sugar and vanilla into a bowl. Beat until light and fluffy. Sift over the flour, add the ground rice and stir in. Gather the dough into a smooth ball.

3. Press into the dish and level the surface. Prick with a fork.

4. Put into the hot oven and cook on 200°C + MED-LOW for about 8–10 minutes or until lightly browned and just firm. Leave to cool on a wire rack.

5. Put the remaining butter, the soft brown sugar and condensed milk into a large bowl. Cook on MED-HIGH for about 5–6 minutes, stirring frequently. The mixture will rise and look thick and curdled. Beat until smooth and glossy.

6. Pour over the shortbread, tipping the dish to make an even layer. Leave until quite cold.

7. Break the chocolate into a small bowl. Cook on MED-HIGH for 1½–2½ minutes, stirring once or twice, or until melted and smooth. Pour evenly over the caramel.

8. Leave until set before cutting into wedges.

BOILED FRUIT CAKE

C

Makes 10–12 slices

225 g/8 oz mixed dried fruit
40 g/1½ oz glacé cherries, chopped
150 g/5¼ oz dark soft brown sugar
225 g/8 oz margarine
1 tsp bicarbonate of soda
1 tsp mixed spice
300 ml/½ pint milk
300 g/10½ oz self-raising flour
2 medium eggs, beaten

1. Put the fruit into a large ovenproof bowl. Add the cherries, sugar, margarine, soda, spice and milk. Cook on HIGH for about 6–8 minutes, stirring once, until the mixture comes to a rolling boil and rises up the bowl. Leave to cool for about 15 minutes.

2. Lightly grease a 20 cm/8 inch ovenproof soufflé dish and line the base with non-stick paper.

3. Sift the flour into the fruit mixture and add the eggs. Mix well. Tip into the dish and level the surface.

4. Cook on 160°C + LOW for about 45–50 minutes or until the cake is cooked (a skewer inserted in the centre should come out clean).

5. Leave to stand for 10 minutes before turning out onto a wire rack to cool completely.

CHERRY AND COCONUT CAKE   C

Makes 8–10 slices

225 g/8 oz self-raising flour
115 g/4 oz butter or block margarine
115 g/4 oz caster sugar
85 g/3 oz desiccated coconut, plus extra for sprinkling
115 g/4 oz glacé cherries
2 medium eggs
150 ml/¼ pint milk
½ tsp almond extract
Glacé cherry halves

1. Preheat the oven to 180°C.

2. Lightly butter an 18 cm/7 inch ovenproof soufflé dish and line the base with non-stick paper.

3. Sift the flour into a bowl and rub in the butter to make coarse crumbs (alternatively, buzz in a food processor). Stir in the sugar and coconut. Finely chop and add the cherries.

4. Lightly beat the eggs with the milk and almond extract. Add to the mixture and beat until well mixed.

5. Tip into the dish and level the surface. Sprinkle with a little extra coconut and arrange cherry halves around the edge.

6. Put into the hot oven and cook on 180°C + LOW for about 22–25 minutes until well risen and golden brown (a skewer inserted in the centre should come out clean).

7. Leave to stand for 10 minutes before turning out on a wire rack to cool.

EASY CRISP PASTRY

No rolling this pastry. Simply press it into the dish and it is ready to cook.

Lines a 20–23 cm/8–9 inch flan dish

175 g/6 oz plain flour
Pinch of salt
Pinch of baking powder
85 g/3 oz chilled butter
1 medium egg, lightly beaten

1. Put the flour, salt and baking powder into a processor and buzz briefly. Cut the butter into small pieces, add to the flour and buzz until the mixture resembles fine breadcrumbs. Add the egg and buzz again until crumbly.

2. Tip the mixture into a lightly greased 20–23 cm/8–9 inch ovenproof flan dish and, with lightly floured fingers, press the dough evenly up the sides and on the base of the dish. Chill for about 30 minutes before cooking.

SWEET EASY CRISP PASTRY

Replace 3 tbsp of the flour with 3 tbsp caster sugar, added to the dry ingredients.

TO COOK UNFILLED PASTRY CASES

Baking blind (cooking a pastry case without its filling) helps to produce a crisp result, particularly on the bottom crust of flans. Chilling an uncooked pastry case for at least 30 minutes helps it to keep its shape. If you brush the inside of the uncooked case with a little beaten egg (could be from the filling), this will help to seal it and to prevent it from absorbing the filling.

For a 20–23 cm/8–9 inch uncooked flan case in an ovenproof flan dish.

1. Preheat the oven to 250°C.

2. If you plan to fill and cook the pastry case again, put the dish into the hot oven and cook on 250°C + LOW for about 5 minutes or until the pastry has set. To cook the pastry completely, put the dish into the hot oven and cook on 250°C + LOW for about 8–10 minutes or until set and lightly browned.

3. Leave to stand for 5 minutes before filling or leave to cool completely.

SODA BREAD

If preferred, use half white and half wholemeal or granary flour.
After sifting the flour, baking powder, soda and salt, add all the bits
remaining in the sieve. Serve, freshly baked, with soup and cheese
or a salad. It is also excellent thickly sliced and toasted.

Serves 6–8

225 g/8 oz plain flour
1½ tsp baking powder
½ tsp bicarbonate of soda
Pinch of salt
25 g/1 oz butter
4 tbsp natural yogurt

1. Preheat the oven to 220°C.

2. Sift the flour, baking powder, soda and salt into a bowl. Rub in
   the butter until the mixture resembles coarse breadcrumbs.

3. Whisk the yogurt into 150 ml/¼ pint cold water and add to the
   bowl. With a round-end knife, mix to form a soft dough. On a
   lightly-floured surface, knead gently until smooth. Shape into a
   ball about 10 cm/4 inches in diameter.

4. Put onto a flat ovenproof plate. Using a large knife, make a deep
   cross in the dough, to make four wedge shapes.

5. Put into the hot oven and cook on 220°C + MED-LOW for about
   14–16 minutes until well risen, crisp and golden brown (a skewer
   inserted in the centre should come out clean).

6. Leave to cool for about 10–15 minutes before serving.

CORIANDER AND
CURRY BREAD

Serve warm with curries or simply as an accompaniment to soup or a light meal.

Serves 4–6

3 tbsp chopped fresh coriander
280 g packet bread or pizza mix
1 tbsp oil
25 g/1 oz butter
2 tsp curry paste

1. Stir the coriander into the bread or pizza mix. Make up the dough, adding the oil to the hand-hot water and following packet instructions.

2. Pat the dough into the base of an oiled ovenproof 23 cm/9 inch flan dish. With a fork, prick all over. Cover with oiled cling film and leave in a warm place to rise for about 30 minutes.

3. Preheat the oven to 220°C.

4. Put the butter and curry paste into a bowl and stand in the warming oven until melted. Stir well. Gently brush the mixture over the risen dough.

5. Put into the hot oven and cook on 220°C + MED-LOW for about 15 minutes or until golden brown and cooked through.

CHEESE AND CHIVE BREAD

Serve warm with soup or a light meal.

Serves 4–6

3 tbsp chopped fresh chives
55 g/2 oz finely grated mature Cheddar cheese
280 g packet bread or pizza mix
1 tbsp oil
25 g/1 oz garlic butter

1. Stir the chives and cheese into the bread or pizza mix. Make up the dough, adding the oil to the hand-hot water and following packet instructions.

2. Pat the dough into the base of an oiled ovenproof 23 cm/9 inch flan dish. With a fork, prick all over. Cover with oiled polythene and leave in a warm place to rise for about 30 minutes.

3. Preheat the oven to 220°C.

4. Put the butter into the warming oven until melted. Gently brush the mixture over the risen dough.

5. Put into the hot oven and cook on 220°C + MED-LOW for about 15 minutes or until golden brown and cooked through.

CHEDDAR AND
WALNUT WEDGES

Serve with soup or as a nibble with drinks.

Makes 8–10 wedges

175 g/6 oz plain flour
Freshly milled salt and pepper
115 g/4 oz chilled butter, cut into cubes
50 g/1¾ oz mature Cheddar cheese, finely grated
50 g/1¾ oz walnuts, finely chopped

1. Lightly grease a 20 cm/8 inch ovenproof flan dish and line the base with non-stick paper. Preheat the oven to 220°C.

2. Sift the flour and seasoning into a bowl, add the butter and rub in with the fingertips until the mixture resembles coarse crumbs (alternatively, buzz in a processor).

3. Stir in the cheese and walnuts and gather the dough into a ball.

4. Tip onto the worktop and knead very lightly until smooth.

5. Press into the dish, levelling the top. Using a fork, mark a border around the edge and prick the centre.

6. Put into the hot oven and cook on 220°C + MED-LOW for about 8–10 minutes or until lightly browned and just firm.

7. Leave to cool for 5 minutes before cutting into wedges. Cool completely before removing from the dish.

9

DESSERTS

Desserts are very easy to make with the help of the combination cooker – the microwaves ensure a good and light texture, while the heat crisps and browns. There is a wide variety of recipes to choose from, Apple Crumb Cake, Plum Crumble Dessert and Orange and Lemon Torte which just need the addition of piping hot custard, crème fraîche or ice-cream.

As mentioned in the cakes, bakes and pastries chapter, before using a recipe, read page 12, regarding the kind of cooking containers to use. If the manufacturer of your cooker recommends the use of metal baking dishes when cooking on combination, do remember that our cooking times have been developed using ovenproof glass containers. The latter allow microwaves to enter the food from all angles to give a successful rise and an even texture – with a shorter cooking time. With metal dishes, you may need to increase the cooking time, and the final texture and appearance may be affected.

Many of the recipes in this chapter are cooked in a preheated (hot) oven – so remember to set your cooker appropriately.

ORANGE AND LEMON TORTE

Serve topped with whipped cream or cut into wedges and serve with fresh fruit salad.

Makes 8–10 slices

2 medium eggs, separated
75 ml/2½ fl oz grapeseed oil
75 ml/2½ fl oz milk
Rind and juice of 1 large lemon
175 g/6 oz plain flour
2 tsp baking powder
280 g/10 oz caster sugar
Finely grated rind and juice of 1 large orange

1. Preheat the oven to 180°C. Lightly grease a deep 20 cm/8 inch ovenproof flan dish and line the base with non-stick paper.

2. To the egg yolks, add the oil, milk and lemon rind and beat until combined. Sift the flour and baking powder into a separate bowl and stir in 150 g/5¹⁄₂ oz of the caster sugar. Add the egg yolk mixture and beat to a smooth batter. Whisk the egg whites to soft peaks and, using a metal spoon, fold into the batter. Pour into the dish and level the top.

3. Put into the hot oven and cook on 180°C + MED-LOW for about 16–18 minutes or until well risen, firm when gently pressed and golden brown. Stand the dish on a wire rack.

4. Put the remaining sugar, lemon and orange juice and the orange rind into a bowl and cook on HIGH for about 2 minutes, stirring once, or until the sugar has dissolved.

5. With a fork, prick the surface of the hot cake and gradually spoon the hot syrup over the top. Leave until quite cold (or overnight).

6. With a round-end knife, loosen the sides of the cake and invert onto a flat serving plate.

APPLE CRUMB CAKE

Good warm or cold with soured cream or ice cream.

Makes 6–8 slices

900 g/2 lb Bramley cooking apples, peeled and sliced
4 tbsp orange juice
6 tbsp clear honey
225 g/8 oz Madeira cake (store-bought)
Finely grated rind and juice of 1 medium lemon
55 g/2 oz flaked almonds
55 g/2 oz sultanas
Icing sugar

1. Put the apples, orange juice and honey into a casserole. Cover (with a vented lid) and cook on HIGH for about 10 minutes, stirring once or twice, until the apples are tender. Beat to a smooth purée.

2. Meanwhile, slice the cake and buzz to crumbs in a processor (or grate it). Put into a bowl with the lemon rind and juice. Mix with a fork until combined. Tip one-third of the crumbs into a small bowl and stir in the almonds. Add the sultanas to the remaining two-thirds.

3. Spoon half of the cake-and-sultana mixture evenly into a 20 cm/ 8 inch ovenproof flan dish. Top with half the apples. Repeat with the remaining crumb-and-sultana mix and the rest of the apple purée. Spoon the crumb-and-almond mixture over the top.

MICROWAVE + GRILL:

4. Stand the dish on a low rack. Cook on MED-LOW + GRILL for about 14–15 minutes or until the top is golden brown.

5. Serve at room temperature or chilled (cool, then cover before refrigerating). Sift a little icing sugar over the top before cutting into wedges.

COMBINATION:

4. Preheat the oven to 200°C.

5. Put into the hot oven and cook on 200°C + MED-LOW for about 19–20 minutes or until the top is golden brown. Cool to room temperature.

6. Serve at room temperature or chilled (cool, then cover before refrigerating). Sift a little icing sugar over the top before cutting into wedges.

CARAMEL BANANA
DESSERT CAKE

Best eaten warm with a scoop of vanilla ice cream or thick natural yogurt.

Makes 6–8 slices

115 g/4 oz soft brown sugar
55 g/2 oz butter
4 ripe medium bananas
115 g/4 oz soft tub margarine
115 g/4 oz caster sugar
2 medium eggs
2 tbsp milk
115 g/4 oz self-raising flour
Pinch of cinnamon

1. Put the brown sugar and butter into a bowl. Cook on HIGH for about 1½–2 minutes, stirring once, until melted. Pour into a 23 cm/9 inch ovenproof flan dish and tip to coat the base of the dish.

2. Slice the bananas thickly on the diagonal and arrange on top of the caramel.

3. Preheat the oven to 220°C.

4. Put the margarine, caster sugar, eggs and milk into a bowl. Sift over the flour and cinnamon. With an electric mixer or wooden spoon, beat until the mixture is smooth and light. Spoon over the top of the bananas levelling the surface.

5. Put into the hot oven and cook on 220°C + MEDIUM for about 10–12 minutes or until the cake is well risen, firm when lightly pressed and golden brown. Leave to stand for at least 10 minutes before serving.

6. Slip a knife around the edge of the cake and invert it onto a warm serving plate. Cut into wedges.

BAKED APPLES

Serve hot with vanilla ice cream or crème fraîche.

To serve 2		To serve 4
2 medium	**Bramley apples**	*4 medium*
	soft butter	
½ tsp	**ground cinnamon**	*1 tsp*
85 g/3 oz	**soft brown sugar**	*175 g/6 oz*

1. Preheat the oven to 200°C.

2. Using a corer and keeping the apples whole, remove the cores. Using a very sharp knife, carefully make a neat cut around the middle of each apple – this allows the apples to expand without bursting as they bake.

3. Generously butter a shallow ovenproof baking dish, just large enough to hold the apples in a single layer. Add the apples. Combine the cinnamon and sugar and pack into the centre of each apple. Top each apple with a generous knob of butter.

4. Put into the hot oven and cook on 200°C + MED-LOW for about 8–10 minutes *(12–15 minutes)* or until the apples are soft in the centre when pierced with a knife. Serve piping hot.

PLUM CRUMBLE DESSERT

If the plums are not very sweet, sprinkle them with a little extra sugar before adding the crumble topping. Serve warm, cut into wedges, with custard or a scoop of ice cream.

Serves 6–8

Topping:
85 g/3 oz self-raising flour
55 g/2 oz chilled butter
55 g/2 oz soft brown sugar
55 g/2 oz coarsely chopped toasted hazelnuts

Cake:
115 g/4 oz self-raising flour
½ tsp ground cinnamon
85 g/3 oz soft tub margarine
85 g/3 oz caster sugar
2 medium eggs, beaten
450 g/1 lb plums, quartered and stoned

1. Preheat the oven to 180°C. Lightly grease a 23 cm/9 inch ovenproof flan dish.

2. Make the topping: Sift the flour into a bowl and rub in the butter to make coarse crumbs. Stir in the sugar and hazelnuts.

3. Make the cake: Sift the flour and cinnamon into a bowl and add the margarine, sugar and eggs. Using a wooden spoon, beat until smooth and creamy. Spoon into the dish and level the surface. Arrange the plums on top and, if wished, sprinkle with a little extra sugar. Spoon the topping evenly over the fruit.

4. Put into the hot oven and cook on 180°C + MED-LOW for about 26–30 minutes or until a skewer inserted in the centre (between the fruit) comes out clean.

5. Leave to cool for about 20 minutes before cutting into wedges for serving.

BUTTERSCOTCH CRUNCH CAKE

As the cake cooks, the crunchy butterscotch topping gently sinks into the batter. Serve warm as dessert, with cream or custard, or cold as cake.

Makes 8–10 slices

85 g/3 oz soft dark brown sugar
55 g/2 oz porridge oats
55 g/2 oz butter, diced
55 g/2 oz chopped mixed nuts
200 g/7 oz caster sugar
115 g/4 oz soft tub margarine
225 ml/8 fl oz Greek-style yogurt
2 medium eggs
1 tsp vanilla extract
250 g/9 oz plain flour
1 tsp baking powder
1 tsp bicarbonate of soda

1. Preheat the oven to 180°C. Line the base of a 23 cm/9 inch ovenproof flan dish with non-stick paper.

2. Put the brown sugar and oats into a bowl, add the butter and rub in with the fingertips to make coarse crumbs. Stir in the nuts.

3. Put the caster sugar, margarine, yogurt, eggs and vanilla into another bowl. Sift over the flour, baking powder and bicarbonate of soda. Using an electric mixer or wooden spoon, beat until the mixture is light and creamy.

4. Spoon into the dish and level the top. Spoon over the topping.

5. Put into the hot oven and cook on 180°C + MED-LOW for about 18–20 minutes or until the cake is golden brown and firm when lightly pressed with a finger.

6. To serve warm, leave to cool slightly before cutting into wedges. To serve cold, leave to cool in the dish on a wire rack for about 30 minutes before turning out onto a plate.

MOCHA DESSERT CAKE
WITH CARAMEL SAUCE $\boxed{\text{C}}$

Makes 8–10 slices

150 g/5½ oz self-raising flour
25 g/1 oz cocoa
175 g/6 oz soft tub margarine
175 g/6 oz soft brown sugar
3 medium eggs
1 tsp vanilla extract
3 tbsp milk
115 g/4 oz granulated sugar
1 tbsp espresso instant coffee granules
2 tbsp coffee liqueur
300 ml/½ pint double or whipping cream

1. Preheat the oven to 200°C. Lightly grease a 23 cm/9 inch ovenproof flan dish and line the base with non-stick paper.

2. Sift the flour and cocoa into a large bowl. Add the margarine, brown sugar, eggs, vanilla and milk. With an electric mixer or wooden spoon, beat until the mixture is smooth and light. Spoon into the dish and level the surface.

3. Put into the hot oven and cook on 200°C + MED-LOW for about 15 minutes or until the cake is well risen and firm when lightly pressed. Stand the dish on a wire rack.

4. Put the granulated sugar and coffee granules into a bowl with 300 ml/½ pint hot water (from the kettle). Heat on HIGH for 2–3 minutes, stirring once, until the sugar has dissolved. Stir in the liqueur.

5. With a fork, pierce the warm cake right through and all over. Slowly spoon the hot syrup evenly over the top. Leave until cold (or overnight).

6. Meanwhile, make the Caramel Sauce (opposite).

7. To serve, turn the cake out onto a serving plate. Softly whip the cream and swirl over the top of the cake. Chill for at least 2 hours. Cut into wedges and serve with the sauce.

CARAMEL SAUCE

140 g/5 oz granulated sugar
15 g/½ oz butter
Finely grated rind and juice of 1 lemon
300 ml/½ pint single cream

1. Put the sugar and 125 ml/4 fl oz cold water into a bowl. Cook on MED-HIGH, without stirring, for 6–8 minutes until a pale golden brown. Leave to stand for 2 minutes.

2. Carefully stir in the butter, lemon rind and juice – take care, the sauce will bubble. Then stir in the cream.

3. Serve at room temperature.

CHERRY FRANGIPANE TART

C

Serve warm or at room temperature.

Makes 6–8 slices

55 g/2 oz soft butter
55 g/2 oz caster sugar
1 medium egg, beaten
55 g/2 oz ground almonds
1 tbsp plain flour, sieved
1 tsp almond extract
2 tsp milk
20 cm/9 inch pre-baked sweet pastry case
425 g can pitted black cherries, drained
Icing sugar

1. Preheat the oven to 220°C.

2. Beat together the butter and sugar until light and fluffy. Gradually beat in the egg. Using a metal spoon, fold in the almonds, flour, almond extract and milk.

3. Arrange the drained cherries in the pastry case and spoon the almond mixture evenly over the top.

4. Put into the hot oven and cook on 220°C + MED-LOW for about 9–10 minutes until the batter is set and the cherries are bubbling.

5. Cool slightly, then sift icing sugar over the top before serving.

MINCEMEAT AND PINEAPPLE CAKE

Best served warm with vanilla ice cream.

Makes 8–10 slices

225 g/8 oz mincemeat
115 g/4 oz dried ready-to eat pineapple

Topping:
75 g/2¾ oz self-raising flour
55 g/2 oz chilled butter
55 g/2 oz brown sugar
½ tsp ground cinnamon
55 g/2 oz pine nuts

Cake:
115 g/4 oz soft butter
115 g/4 oz caster sugar
175 g/6 oz self-raising flour
2 medium eggs, beaten
2–3 tbsp milk
Icing sugar

1. Combine the mincemeat and pineapple.

2. Preheat the oven to 180°C.

3. Make the topping: Sift the flour into a bowl, add the butter and rub in until the mixture resembles coarse crumbs. Stir in the sugar, cinnamon and nuts.

4. Put all the cake ingredients, except the icing sugar, into a bowl and, with an electric mixer or wooden spoon, beat until smooth. Spoon into a 23 cm/9 inch ovenproof flan dish and level the top. Add the mincemeat mixture in small spoonfuls – don't try to spread it evenly. Sprinkle the topping mixture over the mincemeat.

5. Put into the hot oven and cook on 180°C + LOW for about 27–30 minutes or until the cake layer is cooked and the top golden brown.

6. Cool slightly, then sift a little icing sugar over the top before cutting into wedges.

PEAR AND ALMOND SHORTCAKE

Serve warm with a scoop of vanilla ice cream or with soured cream, or serve cold as a cake.

Makes 6–8 slices

200 g/7 oz plain flour
35 g/1¼ oz semolina
150 g/5½ oz chilled butter, diced
70 g/2½ oz soft brown sugar
1 tsp almond extract
Two 411 g cans pear halves, drained
25 g/1 oz flaked almonds
Icing sugar

1. Preheat the oven to 200°C.

2. Put the flour and semolina into a bowl, add the butter and rub in with the fingertips until the mixture looks like breadcrumbs (or buzz in a processor). Stir in the sugar and almond extract.

3. Press three-quarters of the mixture into a 20 cm/8 inch oven-proof dish and level the surface. Cut each pear in half lengthways and arrange on top of the shortbread mixture. Combine the remaining shortbread mixture with the almonds and spoon between the pears.

4. Put into the hot oven and cook on 200°C + MED-LOW for about 18–20 minutes or until lightly brown and just firm. Leave to cool for 5 minutes before sifting a little icing sugar over the top. To serve warm, cut into wedges and serve. To serve cold, cut into wedges and leave to cool completely in the dish.

APRICOT STREUSEL CAKE

Best served warm with single cream.

Makes 8–10 slices

Finely grated rind and juice of 1 large orange
225 g/8 oz dried ready-to-eat apricots

Crumble Topping:
75 g/2¾ oz self-raising flour
50 g/1¾ oz chilled butter
50 g/1¾ oz soft brown sugar
50 g/1¾ oz plain chocolate, coarsely grated

Cake:
115 g/4 oz soft margarine
115 g/4 oz caster sugar
175 g/6 oz self-raising flour
2 medium eggs, beaten
Finely grated rind of 1 orange plus 2–3 tbsp of its juice

1. Put the orange juice and apricots into a casserole. Cover and cook on MED-HIGH for 4 minutes. Leave until cold.

2. Preheat the oven to 180°C.

3. Make the topping: Sift the flour into a bowl, add the butter and rub in until the mixture resembles coarse crumbs. Stir in the sugar and chocolate.

4. Put the cake ingredients into a bowl and, with an electric mixer or wooden spoon, beat until smooth. Spoon into a 23 cm/9 inch ovenproof flan dish and level the top. Arrange the apricots on top. Sprinkle the topping over the fruit.

5. Put into the hot oven and cook on 180°C + LOW for about 27–30 minutes or until the cake layer is cooked and the topping is golden brown.

6. Leave to cool for 10–15 minutes before cutting into wedges.

APPLE CRUMB TART

A new twist to an old favourite. Serve warm with pouring cream, custard or ice cream.

Makes 6–8 slices

225 g/8 oz golden syrup
85 g/3 oz fresh white breadcrumbs
Finely grated rind and juice of 1 large lemon
225 g/8 oz Bramley cooking apple
20 cm/8 inch unbaked pastry case

1. Put the syrup into a bowl and heat on HIGH for 45 seconds until runny. Stir in the breadcrumbs, lemon rind and juice. Leave to stand for 10 minutes.

2. Preheat the oven to 200°C.

3. Peel, core and grate the apple. Stir into the syrup mixture and then spoon it into the pastry case.

4. Cook on 200°C + MED-LOW for about 18–20 minutes or until the pastry is crisp and the filling is golden brown.

5. Cool slightly before cutting into wedges.

INDEX